Conversational
FRENCH
in 7 Days

---

*Master Language Survival Skills
in Just One Week!*

Shirley Baldwin and Sarah Boas

McGraw·Hill

New York   Chicago   San Francisco   Lisbon   London   Madrid   Mexico City
Milan   New Delhi   San Juan   Seoul   Singapore   Sydney   Toronto

Originally published by Hodder & Stoughton Publishers.

4 5 6 7 8 9 0   WKT/WKT   2 1 0 9 8 7 6 5

ISBN 0-07-143251-5 (package)
    0-07-143250-7 (book)

Acknowledgments
The authors and publishers are grateful to the following for supplying photographs or illustrations:
Barnaby's Picture Library (pp. 27, 48)
J. Allan Cash Ltd. (p. 1)
Keith Gibson (pp. 16, 20, 21, 33, 34, 35, 39, 43, 44, 45, 47, 53, 59, 60, 61, 65, 68, 73)
The French Government Tourist Office (pp. 3, 22, 29, 61, 66)
La Régie Autonome des Transports Parisiens (RATP) (pp. 19, 21)

McGraw-Hill books are available at special quantity discounts to use as premiums and sales promotions, or for use in corporate training programs. For more information, please write to the Director of Special Sales, Professional Publishing, McGraw-Hill, Two Penn Plaza, New York, NY 10121-2298. Or contact your local bookstore.

This book is printed on acid-free paper.

CONTENTS

INTRODUCTION

Conversational French in 7 Days is a short course that will equip you to deal with everyday situations when you visit a French-speaking country.

The course is divided into 7 units, each corresponding to a day in the life of Patrick (a designer) and his cousin Claire during their week in France. Each unit begins with a dialogue, which introduces the essential vocabulary in context. The phrasebook section lists these and other useful phrases and defines them in English. Within the units there are also sections giving basic grammatical explanations and a number of practice activities designed to be useful as well as fun. Answers can be checked in the back of the book.

A note about the currency used in this book. In 2002, 12 countries in the European Union, including France, adopted the Euro as the national currency. In this book, the dialogues and text refer to the former currency of France, the *franc*, which is abbreviated as *F* in some of the text and the photos.

Pronunciation

Do stress the last syllable more than the others.
Do run two words together when one word ends in a consonant and the next starts with a vowel: **vous êtes, nous avons**.
Don't pronounce the consonant at the end of a word (*except* those ending in **c,f,l,r**).
Don't pronounce **e** at end of words (*except* in one-syllable words or when it is accented).

Vowels
a as in *father*: va**lise** [vahleez]
a, â as in *baa*: pas [paa]
e as in *sun*: je
e, é, er, ez as in *Spain*: et [ai]
e, è, ê, ai as in *pen*: père [pehr]
e, eu, œ, as in *over*: deux
i as in *feet*: valise
o, ô, eau, au as in *low*: hôtel
o as in *old*: votre [votr]
u as in *few*: une [ewn], numéro
ou as in *loot*: tout [too]

Nasalized vowels
am/an like *taunt*: grand [grah(n)]
em/en   en [ah(n)]
im/in   fin [fa(n)]
ain/ein   pain [pa(n)]
om/on   bon [boh(n)]
um/un like *earnest*: lundi
        [luh(n)dee]
Semi-vowels
ui like *sweet*: oui [wee]
oi/oy like *swan*: moi [mwa]
ll like *yet*: cuiller [kwee-yer]
ail like *pie*: travail [tra-vye]

Consonants: similar to English but with the following exceptions:
c before *i* or *e* like *sun*: c'est
ç always like *sun*: ça
ch like *shun*: chant
g before *i* or *e* like *leisure*: voyage
gn like *union*: montagne
h always silent: l'hôtel [lotel]
j like *leisure*: je
qu like *can*: quarante
r tongue at back of mouth; merci

SAYING HELLO AND GOODBYE

▶ **Arrival**   When arriving at a port or airport, you will find customs and passport procedures standard and easy to follow, because most information is given in English as well as in French. You should check duty free allowances before setting out on your trip. Look out for the sign DOUANE (*Customs*).

l'arrivée/the arrival

Patrick and his cousin Claire are traveling to France together. They disembark at the hoverport.

"Mesdames et Messieurs, nous vous remercions d'avoir voyagé avec nous et espérons vous revoir bientôt à bord." (*Ladies and gentlemen, thank you for traveling with us. We hope to have you on board again soon.*)

Hôtesse:	(to Patrick and Claire) **Au revoir et bon voyage, monsieur-madame**.
Patrick et Claire:	Au revoir, mademoiselle et merci.

Patrick (22, director of a small design firm, is met by his French agent, Bernard Rousseau.

Bernard:	**Bonjour, monsieur. Vous êtes M. Vincent?**
Patrick:	**Oui, je m'appelle** Patrick Vincent.
Bernard:	**Je me présente.** Je suis Bernard Rousseau.
Patrick:	**Ah, bonjour** Bernard. **Enchanté de faire votre connaissance.**
Bernard:	Donnez-moi votre valise, s'il vous plaît. La voiture est là-bas. L'hôtel est tout près.
Patrick:	Merci beaucoup.

Clair (17) is met by the French family she is going to stay with.

Mme Bergeron:	**C'est vous,** Claire Rogers?
Claire:	**Oui, c'est moi.**
Mme Bergeron:	**Je suis** Madame Bergeron, **et voici** mon fils, Julien. **Comment ça va?** Vous avez fait un bon voyage?
Claire:	Oui, très bien merci, madame.
Julien:	Dépêchons-nous, maman. Le taxi attend.
Mme Bergeron:	Eh bien, Julien, prends les bagages.

▶ ▶ ▶ **Saying hello and goodbye**   In France, people generally shake hands each time they meet and when saying goodbye. Always address a man as **monsieur**, and a woman as **madame**, or **mademoiselle** for a young girl or if you know she is not married.

Bonjour, monsieur.	Hello (to a man).
Bonsoir, madame.	Good evening (to a woman).
Salut! Comment ça va?	Hello! (to a friend) How are things?
Ça va bien, merci.	Fine, thanks.
Comment allez-vous?	How are you?
Très bien, merci.	Very well, thank you.

Introducing yourself

Je m'appelle . . .	My name is . . .
Je me présente . . . Je suis . . .	Let me introduce myself . . . I am . . .
Voici mon fils/mon mari/ma femme.	Here is my son/my husband/my wife.
Enchanté* de faire votre connaissance.	Pleased to meet you.
C'est vous, . . . ?/Vous êtes . . . ?	Are you . . . ?
Oui, c'est moi.	Yes, it's me.
Oui/Non	Yes/No

   * **Enchantée** for a woman.

Saying goodbye

Au revoir.	Good-bye.
A bientôt.	See you soon.
A tout à l'heure.	See you later.
A plus tard.	See you later.

Saying please and thank you

S'il vous plaît	Please
Merci.	Thank you.
Merci beaucoup.	Thank you very much.
De rien.	You're welcome.
Il n'y a pas de quoi.	Don't mention it.

USEFUL WORDS AND PHRASES

Donnez-moi la valise.	Give me the suitcase.
La voiture est là-bas.	The car is over there.
L'hôtel est tout près.	The hotel is nearby.
Vous avez fait un bon voyage?	Did you have a good trip?
Dépêchons-nous, maman!	Let's hurry, Mom!
Le taxi attend.	The taxi is waiting.
Eh bien	Well
Prends les bagages.	Take the luggage.

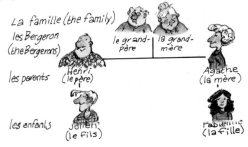

La famille (the family)
les Bergeron (the Bergerons)
les parents
les enfants
le grand-père
la grand-mère
Henri (le père)
Agathe (la mère)
Julien (le fils)
Fabienne (la fille)

the way it works

People and things

In French, words for both people and things are masculine or feminine. There is no sure way of guessing which is which, and the gender of each noun must simply be learned. The word for "the" is **le** before a masculine noun—**le fils, le taxi**—and **la** before a feminine noun—**la voiture, la valise**. Use **l'** before masculine and feminine words beginning with a vowel and most words beginning with **h: l'arrivée, l'hôtel.**

For more than one thing use **les**—**les bagages, les passagers.**

If you want to say "a" in French, use **un** before a masculine noun—**un voyage, un départ**—and **une** before a feminine noun—**une valise, une traversée.**

I am, you are

Je suis Patrick Vincent.	I am Patrick Vincent.
Vous êtes M. Vincent.	You are Mr. Vincent.

The word for "you" in French is normally **vous**, but with people you know well and with members of the family and children, use the word **tu.**
Tu es = you are (familiar)

Mine and yours

To say "my" in French, use **mon** for a masculine noun—**mon fils**, **mon sac**; and **ma** for a feminine noun—**ma fille**, **ma sœur**. For words in the plural, "my " is **mes**: **mes parents**, **mes compliments**.

To say "your" in French, use **votre** for singular masculine and feminine nouns— **votre frère**, **votre sœur**; and **vos** for nouns in the plural—**vos bagages**, **vos enfants**. However, when talking to members of the family or close friends use **ton**, **ta** or **tes** instead of **votre**: **ton frère**, **ta sœur**, **tes parents**.

Note: for masculine and feminine nouns beginning with a vowel or **h** use **mon**, **ton**: **mon arrivée**, **ton hôtel**.

The full list of possessive adjectives is on p. 10.

things to do

1.1 Practice saying hello and goodbye to the following people, not forgetting to add **monsieur**, **madame**, **mademoiselle** as appropriate.

   1 Mr. Dupont (a business colleague)

   2 Mrs. Le Gros (a shopkeeper)

   3 Mrs. Maury (a friend of your mother)

   4 Clothilde (a waitress)

   5 Damien (a friend)

1.2 Complete the following exchanges in which meetings are taking place:

   1 Mme Leclerc: Bonjour madame. Vous êtes Madame Valéry?
      Mme Valéry: Oui . . .
   2 Employé: Bonjour monsieur/madame. Votre nom, s'il vous plaît?
      Vous:
   3 Mme Ricard: Je me présente. Je suis Madame Ricard.
      Vous:
   4 Mme Maury: Bonjour Robert. Comment allez-vous?
      Robert:
   5 Antoine: Salut André! Comment ca va?
      André:

1.3 Is it yours? Reply, saying, "Yes it is." Use **mon**, **ma** or **mes**.
   1 C'est votre valise, monsieur?   **5** C'est votre nom, monsieur?
   2 C'est votre taxi, madame?   **6** Ce sont vos bagages, madame?
   3 C'est votre voiture, madame?   **7** C'est votre passeport, monsieur?
   4 C'est votre fils, monsieur?

RESERVING ACCOMMODATIONS

Accommodations There are five categories of hotel, with a rating of up to four stars. Prices are posted up in the **réception** and on the backs of the bedroom doors, and are usually quoted for two—although prices may be the same irrespective of the number of occupants. Prices do not usually include breakfast. Hotel guests may be asked to fill out a registration form (**une fiche**) on arrival, giving details of nationality, passport number, and so on. **Pensions** are similar to boarding houses, and **auberges** to country inns. **Logis de France** are reasonably priced country hotels, and **relais de campagne** are more expensive country inns. The tourist office (**le syndicat d'initiative**) in each town keeps a list of hotels as well as rooms in private homes.

Gîtes de France offer cheap self-catering accommodations outside the cities and are extremely popular.

Youth hostels (**Auberges de jeunesse**) are also very popular in summer, when it is essential to reserve in advance. Details of maximum length of stay, which may be only 3 days or up to a week, are available from the International Youth Hostel Handbook.

à l'hôtel/at the hotel

Patrick and Bernard check in at the hotel. Patrick has reserved a room.

Réceptionniste:	Bonjour, messieurs.
Patrick:	Bonjour, Madame. **J'ai réservé une chambre pour deux nuits.**
Réceptionniste:	Oui, monsieur. C'est à quel nom?
Patrick:	**Au nom de M. Vincent.**
Réceptionniste:	Ah oui, M. Vincent. Votre chambre est le numéro neuf au deuxième étage. Voulez-vous remplir cette fiche, s'il vous plaît?
Patrick:	Oui, madame, volontiers.

(He fills in the form.)

Réceptionniste:	Merci, monsieur. Voilà votre clé.

Bernard, whose wife Martine (a teacher) is joining him later in the day, also wants a room for the night, but he hasn't reserved in advance.

Bernard:	Moi aussi, **je voudrais une chambre pour ce soir**, s'il vous plaît, madame.
Réceptionniste:	Oui, monsieur. Pour combien de personnes?
Bernard:	**Pour deux personnes.**
Réceptionniste:	Il y a une très belle chambre à deux lits avec salle de bains au premier étage . . . Nous avons aussi une petite chambre à un grand lit avec douche au troisième étage.
Bernard:	Bon, alors la chambre avec salle de bains, **c'est combien?**
Réceptionniste:	Le prix de la chambre est de 500 francs, monsieur.
Bernard:	**Mais c'est trop cher!** Je prends la petite chambre.
Réceptionniste:	Très bien, monsieur. Voici la clé. C'est le numéro treize . . .

Camping Camping is only permitted at officially designated sites, lists of which can be obtained from the French Government Tourist Office, as well as the various handbooks. Campgrounds have a one- to four-star rating, and the larger ones have many amenities, such as restaurants, supermarkets, heated pools and sports facilities. Tents, trailers, and cabins can be rented at many sites. Camping is very popular, and it is essential to reserve well in advance for the summer months.

au camping/at the campground

The Bergeron family are taking Claire camping with them. They arrive at the campground where they have reserved a spot. Henri Bergeron, the father, is talking to the campground manager.

Henri:	Bonjour, monsieur. Je suis M. Bergeron. **J'ai réservé un emplacement pour huit jours.**
Gardien:	Oui, monsieur. Votre emplacement est là-bas, sous ces arbres. La piscine est à côté.
Agathe B.:	Mais c'est parfait! Nous dressons les tentes tout de suite, les enfants . . .
Henri:	Julien, où est le réchaud?
Julien:	Je ne sais pas, papa. Il n'est pas dans la voiture.
Henri:	Ah non! J'ai laissé le réchaud à la maison.
Agathe:	Qu'est ce qu'il y a, chéri? Tu ne trouves pas le réchaud? Quelle tête en l'air! Ça ne fait rien, ce soir nous achetons des plats cuisinés!

Getting a room at a hotel

Chambres à louer	Rooms for rent
J'ai réservé une chambre.	I have reserved a room.
Vous avez une chambre libre?	Do you have a room free?
Je voudrais une chambre . . .	I would like a room . . .
pour ce soir	for this evening
pour le weekend	for the weekend
pour deux nuits	for two nights
pour huit jours ⎫	for a week
pour une semaine ⎭	
à un lit/à deux lits/à un grand lit	with single bed/twin beds/double bed
avec salle de bains/douche/	with a bathroom/shower/toilet/
cabinet de toilette (WC)/balcon	balcony
au rez-de-chaussée	on the first floor
au premier étage	on the second floor
C'est à quel nom?	What name is it?
C'est au nom de . . .	It's in the name of . . .
Pour combien de personnes?	For how many?
Votre chambre est le numéro neuf.	Your room is no. 9.
Voulez-vous remplir cette fiche?	Will you fill out this form?
chambre d'hôte	bed and breakfast
en pension/en demi-pension	full board/half board
la réception	reception
l'escalier/l'ascenseur	stairs/elevator
Il y a une très belle chambre.	There's a very nice room.
Nous avons aussi une petite chambre.	We also have a small room.
Puis-je voir la chambre?	Can I see the room?

7

At the hotel

La clé du (cinq), s'il vous plaît.	The key to room (five), please.
Voilà votre clé.	Here's your key.
Puis-je avoir un oreiller?/du savon?	Can I have a pillow?/some soap?
une serviette de bain?	a bath towel?
encore une couverture?	another blanket?
La lumière ne marche pas.	The light doesn't work.
La douche . . .	The shower . . .
La note, s'il vous plaît.	The bill, please.
Est-ce que le service est compris?	Is service included?
Je crois qu'il y a une erreur.	I think there is a mistake.

Reserving a campsite

Est-ce qu'il y a un camping près d'ici?	Is there a campground near here?
Avez-vous un emplacement?	Do you have a free site?
J'ai réservé un emplacement.	I have reserved a site.
Votre emplacement est là-bas	Your site is over there
. . . sous ces arbres.	. . . under those trees.
La piscine est à côté.	The swimming pool is nearby.
C'est pour une tente/pour une caravane.	It's for a tent/for a trailer.
C'est combien par nuit?	How much is it per night?
Y a-t-il de l'eau potable?	Is there drinking water?
un magasin sur place?	a shop on the site?
un restaurant?/une laverie?	a restaurant?/a laundry?
une piscine?	a swimming pool?
Nous dressons les tentes tout de suite.	We'll put up the tents at once.
Nous achetons des plats cuisinés.	We'll buy carryout food.

Prices

C'est combien?	How much is it?
Quel est le tarif?	What are the rates?
Quel est le prix de la chambre?	What is the price of the room?
Le prix est de . . .	The price is . . .
C'est trop cher!	It's too expensive!
Je prends la petite chambre.	I'll take the little room.

USEFUL WORDS AND PHRASES

volontiers	of course, willingly
Bon, alors	Good (then)
Voici . . .	Here is
C'est parfait!	It's perfect!
Où est le réchaud?	Where is the stove?
Je ne sais pas.	I don't know.
Il n'est pas dans la voiture.	It isn't in the car.
J'ai laissé . . . à la maison.	I have left . . . at home.
Qu'est-ce qu'il y a, chéri?	What's the matter, darling?
Tu ne trouves pas . . . ?	Can't you find . . . ?
Ça ne fait rien.	It doesn't matter.
Quelle tête en l'air!	What a scatterbrain!

Camping signs

location de tentes	tent rental
eau potable	drinking water
bloc sanitaire	washhouse
défense de laver la vaisselle dans les lavabos	no dish washing in the sinks
parking obligatoire	compulsory parking
réservé aux caravanes	trailers only
interdiction de camper ici	no camping here
caravaning interdit	no trailers allowed
complet	full

CAMPING "DES SABLES DORES"
rue du Port, S. JEAN-SUR-MER

Terrain ouvert du 13 mai au 30 septembre.
Possibilité de réservation.

Bureau de réception
Camp office

Camp gardé
Camp supervised

Branchement électrique pour caravanes **Electricity hookups for trailers**	Prises pour rasoirs électriques **Outlets for electric razors**

Eau chaude pour douches **Hot water for showers**	Lavoirs **Washhouses**	Table à repasser **Ironing table**

Ping-pong **Table tennis**	Balançoire **Swing**	Piscine **Swimming pool**	Distribution du courrier **Postal service**

Dépot de camping gaz **Propane gas on sale**	Ravitaillement au camp **Stores at the camp**

DISTANCES
Restaurant à 500 m
Plage des sables dorés à 4 km
Canotage, voile ou yachting   3 km 500

Ecole équitation   à 1 km
Pêche en rivière   à 200 m du camp
Casino, cinéma, tennis à 3 km

the way it works

At

The word for "at" in French is **à**: **à** Paris. Its form changes depending on whether it is followed by a masculine, feminine or plural noun: **au restaurant**, **à la maison**, **aux magasins**. Before a noun beginning with a vowel or **h** use **à l'**: **à l'hôtel** (at the hotel).

This and that

The word for "this" or "that" is **ce** for a masculine word (**ce soir** = this evening), **cette** for a feminine word (**cette fiche** = this form), **cet** for a masculine word beginning with a vowel or **h** (**cet arbre** = this tree, **cet hôtel** = this hotel), and **ces** for a word in the plural (**ces arbres** = these trees).

It is

C'est means "it is": **c'est trop cher** = it's too expensive. But if you are talking about something in particular, use **il** or **elle** for that thing: **il est dans la voiture**, it (e.g., the stove) is in the car.

I, you, he, etc. (subject pronouns)

Here is a complete list of the subject pronouns:

I	**je**	we	**nous**
you (singular)	**tu**	you (plural)	**vous**
he/it	**il**	they	**ils**
she/it	**elle**	they	**elles**

His, her, its, etc. (possessive adjectives)

The complete list is as follows:

masc.	fem.	pl.		masc.	fem.	pl.	
mon	**ma**	**mes**	my	**notre**	**notre**	**nos**	our
ton	**ta**	**tes**	your (familiar)	**votre**	**votre**	**vos**	your
son	**sa**	**ses**	his/her/its	**leur**	**leur**	**leurs**	their

Verbs

The verb **trouver** means "to find," and many French verbs have endings like **trouver**. It is worth spending some time learning these endings.

je trouv**e**	I find	nous trouv**ons**	we find
tu trouv**es**	you find	vous trouv**ez**	you find
il trouv**e**	he, it finds	ils trouv**ent**	they find (masc.)
elle trouv**e**	she, it finds	elles trouv**ent**	they find (fem.)

Remember to use the **tu** form of "you" when speaking to a child or close friend, and the **vous** form when speaking to someone you don't know or more than one person.

Adjectives

Adjectives in French change their endings depending on whether the noun is masculine or feminine:
un petit lit = a small bed BUT **une petite chambre** = a small room
un grand camping = a big campsite BUT **une grande tente** = a big tent

Negatives

If you want to say "No, it isn't," "No I don't," etc., simply put **ne** before the verb and **pas** after the verb:

Je **ne** sais **pas**.	I don't know.
Il **n**'est **pas** dans la voiture.	It isn't in the car.

1.4 Practice reserving different sorts of hotel rooms.

1   Je voudrais une chambre avec . . .

2   Je voudrais . . .

3   Je voudrais . . .

4   Je voudrais . . .

5   Je voudrais . . .

6   Je voudrais . . .

Now practice reserving for your friend who wants a room with a lot of extras (double bed, shower, and toilet). Elle voudrait . . .

1.5 Where are the following objects? You think they are in the obvious place.

1 Où est le réchaud? Dans la voiture?
Oui, le réchaud est dans la voiture.

2 Où est la valise? Dans le coffre? (trunk of car)

3 Où est la clé? Dans la porte? (door)

4 Où est la tente? Sous les arbres?

5 Où est la douche? Dans la salle de bains?

6 Où est le passeport? Dans le sac? (bag)

1.6 But none of these things is where you thought it was. This time use **il** or **elle** for "it."

1 Le réchaud? Non, il n'est pas dans la voiture.

2 La valise? Non, elle . . .

3 La clé? Non, elle . . .

4 La tente? Non, elle . . .

5 La douche? Non, elle . . .

6 Le passeport? Non, il . . .

1.7 Will everything fit in the car? Your friends are anxious to know if your belongings will take up too much room. You reassure them.

1 Tu as une grande tente?
Non, elle est petite.

2 Tu as une grande valise?
Non, . . .

3 Tu as un grand sac de couchage? (sleeping bag)

4 Tu as un grand réchaud?

5 Tu as un grand sac?

1.8 You are with a group of people staying at a hotel.
Tell the others what room numbers they have been allocated, and on what floor. (See p. 80 for a list of numbers.)

1 Alexandre: room 7 on the third floor.
Alexandre, vous avez la chambre numéro sept au troisième étage.

2 François: room 5 on the third floor

3 Nathalie: room 10 on the second floor.

4 Christian: room 2 on the first floor (au rez-de-chaussée).

5 Florence: room 14 on the fourth floor.

ORDERING BREAKFAST

Breakfast in France is a light meal usually consisting of bread and butter, and sometimes croissants or rolls, and is served with freshly made coffee.

le petit déjeuner à l'hôtel/breakfast at the hotel

Before setting out for the design exhibition in Paris, Patrick Vincent and Martine Rousseau are having breakfast in the hotel. Patrick calls the waiter.

Patrick:	**Garçon, s'il vous plaît!**
	(he turns to Martine) Mais, où est Bernard? Il est déjà neuf heures.
Martine:	Il se renseigne sur le départ des trains pour Paris.
Garçon:	Vous prenez, monsieur-madame?
Martine:	**Moi, je prends un jus d'orange et un yaourt nature.**
Patrick:	**Et pour moi du thé, du pain et des croissants avec de la confiture.** Ah, voilà Bernard qui arrive . . .
Garçon;	(turns to Bernard) Et pour vous, monsieur?
Bernard:	**Apportez-moi un café noir, s'il vous plaît.**
Garçon:	C'est tout? Très bien, madame-messieurs.
Martine:	Le train pour Paris part à quelle heure?
Bernard:	Il faut se dépêcher, mes amis. Le train part dans une demi-heure.

Ordering breakfast

Garçon, s'il vous plaît!	Waiter!
Vous prenez, monsieur-madame?	What would you like?
Moi, je prends un jus d'orange/un yaourt nature.	I'd like an orange juice/a plain yogurt.
Et pour moi . . .	And for me . . .
du thé/du café/du chocolat	tea/coffee/hot chocolate
du pain/des croissants	bread/croissants
avec de la confiture	with jam
et du beurre	and butter
Apportez-moi un café noir/un café au lait.	Bring me a black coffee/coffee with milk.
C'est tout?	Anything else?
Vous avez des croissants?	Do you have croissants?

USEFUL WORDS AND PHRASES

déjà	already
Voilà (Bernard) qui arrive	Here comes (Bernard).
Très bien	Very good
Il faut se dépêcher, mes amis.	We must hurry, my friends.

FRENCH RAILWAYS

French Railways   The *SNCF* (The French railroad company) runs a modern and efficient service. All the main railway lines radiate out from Paris. Types of trains include the following:

TEE	Trans-Europ-Express. Fast international service, first-class only.
TGV	Train à grande vitesse. High-speed inter-city service. Selected routes.
Rapide	Fast, long-distance express linking main cities.
Express	Slower long-distance train.
Omnibus	Local stopping train.
Autorail	Short-haul diesel.

Reserve in advance for long-distance trips and check the bargain fares available on certain days of the week. In general children under 4 travel free and under 10 travel at half fare. When you have bought your ticket, don't forget to validate (**composter**) it in the date-stamping machine at the entrance to the platform (see p. 16).

au guichet/at the ticket window

Sylvie, a colleague of Bernard, is at the Rouen train station buying a ticket to Paris.

Sylvie:	**Je voudrais un billet pour Paris, s'il vous plaît.**
Employé:	Oui, madame, un aller simple ou un aller-retour?
Sylvie:	**Un aller simple, s'il vous plaît.**
Employé:	En première ou seconde classe?
Sylvie:	**En seconde.**
Employé:	Voilà, madame, ça fait quatre-vingts francs.
Sylvie:	Merci, monsieur. Dites-moi, **à quelle heure part le prochain train?**
Employé:	A 12 h 17, madame. C'est le quai numéro 3. Vous avez juste cinq minutes!

A la gare (at the train station)

Accès aux quais	This way to platforms
Consigne (automatique)	Short-term baggage storage (lockers)
Défense de fumer	No smoking
Départ	Departures
Arrivée	Arrivals
Bureau de renseignements	Information office
Salle d'attente	Waiting room
Grandes lignes	Long-distance trains
Trains de banlieue	Suburban trains
l'Horaire SNCF	Train schedule
Wagon-Restaurant	Restaurant car
Wagon-lit	Sleeping car

DÉFENSE DE FUMER

WAGON-LIT   **ARRIVÉE**

DÉPART   **QUAI 4**

What time is it?

... HEURES   ... HEURES ET QUART

Quelle heure est-il?	What time is it?
Il est neuf heures.	It's nine o'clock.
. . . neuf heures cinq	. . . five after nine
. . . neuf heures un (or et) quart	. . . a quarter after nine
. . . neuf heures et demie	. . . nine thirty
. . . neuf heures moins le quart	. . . a quarter to nine
. . . neuf heures moins dix	. . . ten to nine
du matin/de l'après-midi/du soir	in the morning/afternoon/evening

... HEURES MOINS LE QUART   ... HEURES ET DEMIE

Train information

Renseignements	Information
Il se renseigne sur . . .	He is finding out about . . .
. . . le départ des trains pour Paris	. . . departure times of trains to Paris
Il part à quelle heure, le train pour Paris?/de Paris?	What time does the Paris train leave?
A quelle heure est le prochain train?	What time is the next train?
Il part a dix-sept heures quinze.	It leaves at 17:15.
. . . dans cinq minutes	. . . in five minutes
. . . dans une demi-heure	. . . in half an hour
. . . à midi/à minuit	. . . at noon/at midnight
Il faut combien de temps . . . ?	How long does it take . . . ?
. . . pour aller de Boulogne à Paris?	to go from Boulogne to Paris?
Il faut deux heures.	It takes two hours.
Il arrive à quelle heure?	When does it arrive?
Il arrive à . . .	It arrives at . . .
aujourd'hui/demain/hier	today/tomorrow/yesterday
C'est quelle ligne pour . . . ?	What train do you take for . . . ?
Est-ce qu'il y a une correspondance?	Do you have to change trains?
Non, c'est direct.	No, it's direct.
Oui, il faut changer à Vichy.	Yes, you have to change at Vichy.

Buying a ticket

le guichet	ticket window
Je voudrais un billet.	I want a ticket.
pour Paris	for Paris
un aller simple/un aller-retour	a one-way/round-trip ticket
en première/deuxième classe	first/second class
le quai numéro trois	platform 3
tarif réduit	reduced fare
la réservation	reservation

At the train station, listen for the following phrases in announcements:

le train en direction de/à destination de . . .	. . . the train for . . .
le train en provenance de . . .	the train from . . .
en retard/à l'avance	late/early
voie quatre	track 4

USEFUL WORDS AND PHRASES

Voilà   There you are   **Dites-moi**   Tell me

the way it works

To make a noun plural

When talking about more than one thing, you use **les** instead of **le/la/l'** and
normally you add **s** to the noun:
le croissant; **les** croissant**s**
la valise; **les** valise**s**
l'heure; **les** heure**s**

However, a few nouns add **x** instead or change **-al** to **-aux**:
le château; les château**x** (castles), le journal; les journ**aux** (newspapers).

How to say "some" or "any"

Note the following phrase from the first dialogue: **Du** thé, **du** pain et **des** croissants,
avec **de la** confiture. If you want to say "some":
Use **du** with a masculine word: **du** thé, **du** pain
      de la with a feminine word: **de la** confiture
      des with a plural word: **des** croissants
With a word starting with a vowel or **h**, use **de l'**: **De l'**eau, s'il vous plaît (Some
water, please).

Telling the time

Always state the hour before the minutes.

Il est trois heures dix.   It is ten after three.
Il est dix heures moins vingt.   It is twenty to ten.

Official French time always uses the twenty-four hour clock.
Il est treize heures (13h00).   It is 13:00 hours (1:00 p.m.)
(**h** is short for **heures** but it is usually omitted in timetables.)

In less official use and in speech, use the twelve-hour clock.
To specify the time of day, you can add: **du matin/de l'après-midi/du soir.**

Adverbs

In French most adverbs are formed by adding **-ment** to the feminine form of an adjective:
lente (slow)   lente**ment** (slowly)
heureuse (happy)   heureuse**ment** (happily)

To be and to have

Here are two very common verbs which do not follow the normal patterns:
être *to be*

je **suis**	I am	nous **sommes**	we are
tu **es**	you are	vous **êtes**	you are
il **est**	he, it is	ils **sont**	they are
elle **est**	she, it is	elles **sont**	they are

avoir *to have*

j'**ai**	I have	nous **avons**	we have
tu **as**	you have	vous **avez**	you have
il **a**	he, it has	ils **ont**	they have
elle **a**	she, it has	elles **ont**	they have

Asking questions

If you want to ask a question there are several ways of doing it in French:
Vous avez des œufs.   You have some eggs.
Vous avez des œufs? (*with questioning tone*)
Avez-vous des œufs?   Do you have any eggs?
Est-ce que vous avez des œufs?

things to do

2.1 The waiter is taking orders for breakfast.
Vous prenez, messieurs-dames?
Each member of your party wants something different.
What might they say?
Example: Denise: Je voudrais du café.

1 Catherine: 2 Lucien: 3 Nadine:

4 Olivier: 5 André:

2.2 *Quelle heure est-il?* Someone asks you the time. But it seems that the watches of each member of your party say different times, e.g., Il est trois heures.

1   2   3   4   5   6

2.3 *Au guichet des reinseignements*/At the information window
You overhear the ticket agent advising a passenger about trains. Can you guess what the passenger is asking?

Passenger: . . . .
Agent: Le prochain train pour Paris part à neuf heures trente.
Passenger: . . . .
Agent: Il faut environ deux heures et demie por aller de Boulogne à Paris.
Passenger: . . . .
Agent: Il arrive à onze heurs cinquante-cinq.
Passenger: . . . .
Agent: Non, c'est direct.

2.4 Buying a ticket. You are at a ticket office in Paris with a party of tourists, several of whom want to go to different places. Since you are the only one who speaks French, you have to buy the tickets. The first one is done for you.

1 Katy: *Round-trip ticket to Vichy, second class.* Elle voudrait un billet aller-retour à Vichy, en deuxième classe.
2 Mike: *One-way to Lyon, first class.*
3 Stuart and Alison: *Round-trip to Avignon, second class.* (Ils voudraient . . .)
4 Peter: *Round-trip to Bordeaux, second class.*
5 John and Sue: *One-way to Nice, first class.*

TRAVELING BY PUBLIC TRANSPORTATION

▶ **Le métro** The subway in Paris is called the **Métro**. It is a cheap way to travel in Paris and the network is very extensive (see map). In the city you pay a flat fare however many stations you travel. If you plan on using the Métro a lot, it is worth buying a book of tickets, called a **carnet**, or, for short visits, it is worth finding out about the one-day Mobilis pass or the multi-day Paris Visite pass, which you can use on other forms of public transportation as well.

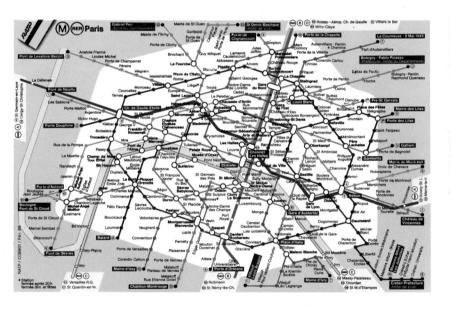

dans le métro/in the metro

Patrick and Bernard have arrived in Paris. They want to go to the Paris-Nord Convention Center at Roissy and look at the metro map to find out how to get there.

Patrick: **Pour aller à l'Exposition**, voyons . . .

Bernard: Regardons le plan du métro. **Nous prenons le RER direction Roissy, et nous descendons au Parc des Expositions.**

Martine: Vous allez passer tout l'après-midi à Roissy?

Barnard: Oui, bien sûr. L'exposition ouvre demain matin et nous devons rencontrer des collègues.

Martine: Bon. Dans ce cas-là, je vous laisse, mes amis. Moi, je vais rejoindre une amie, et après je vais dans les grands magasins. Je cherche de nouvelles chaussures et une jupe, et à Paris—il faut en profiter.

Bernard: Alors, chérie, n'oublie pas d'acheter des petits cadeaux pour les enfants.

Traveling on the métro

Où se trouve la station de métro?	Where is the subway station?
Regardons le plan du métro.	Let's look at the metro map.
Prenons le RER.	We'll take the RER.
direction Roissy	going to Roissy
Nous descendons au Parc des Expositions.	We get off at Convention Center.
un ticket (de métro)	subway ticket
un carnet de tickets	book of tickets

▷ **Le RER**   The fastest means of crossing Paris, this network consists of four lines and extends outward to the suburbs. Although the flat-fare system applies as on the Métro in the middle of Paris, fares vary according to the length of journey into the suburbs.

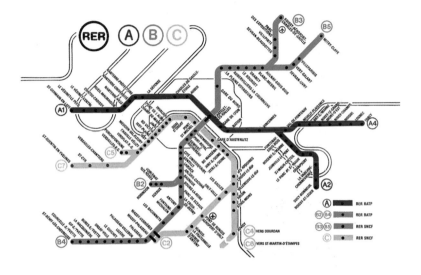

▷ **L'autobus**   A map of the bus system can be found at all bus shelters, in Métro stations, or at any tourist office. On most buses, you can purchase a ticket on board or use a Métro ticket, Mobilis, or Visite pass.

▷ **Le taxi**   To find a taxi go to a taxi stand. There are often set fares between main train stations. You should expect to have to pay a set charge for you and your luggage (**la prise en charge**) and to give a tip (**un pourboire**) of 10–15% to the driver.

FINDING YOUR WAY

pour aller à la plage?/how do we get to the beach?

Julien and Claire want to go to the beach. They ask a policeman (**un gendarme**) the best way to get there.

Julien:	**Excusez-moi, monsieur, la plage c'est loin d'ici?**
Gendarme:	Non, c'est tout près; vous avez dix minutes à pied. Attendez, je vais vous montrer sur le plan. Nous sommes ici, n'est-ce pas? Vous tournez à gauche dans la rue du Port. Vous continuez tout droit et à cent mètres vous prenez la petite rue à droite, la rue de la Plage . . .
Julien:	. . . mais, c'est trop difficile. **Est-ce qu'il y a un autobus?**
Gendarme:	Oui, l'arrêt d'autobus est juste en face du camping. Mais les bus ne sont pas très fréquents. Ils passent toutes les deux heures.
Claire:	Bon, moi **je vais à la plage à pied**. Tu viens avec moi, Julien?
Julien:	Non. Allons demander à Papa de nous y emmener en voiture.
Claire:	Comme tu es paresseux!

How do I get there?

Excusez-moi, monsieur . . .	Excuse me, sir . . .
la plage c'est loin d'ici?	is the beach far from here?
Pour aller à . . . ?	How do I get to . . . ?
Où est . . . Où se trouve . . . ?	Where is . . . ?
Pardon, monsieur, le (terrain de) camping?	Excuse me, where is the campground?
C'est loin d'ici?	Is it far from here?

Non, c'est tout près.	No, it's very near.
c'est assez près/assez loin	it's quite near/quite far
Je vous montre sur le plan.	I'll show you on the map.
Nous sommes ici.	We are here.
Vous tournez à gauche/à droite.	Turn left/right.
la rue du Port	Harbor Street
Continuez tout droit. ⎫ Allez tout droit. ⎭	Go straight ahead.
à cent mètres	after 100 meters
Vous prenez la petite rue à droite.	Take the little street on the right.
jusqu'à	as far as
C'est juste en face.	It's right across the street.
Prenez la première rue à gauche.	Take the first street on the left.
C'est la troisième rue à droite.	It's the third street on the right.
Vous avez vingt minutes à pied.	It's 20 minutes on foot.
Est-ce qu'il y a un autobus?	Is there a bus?
L'arrët d'autobus est juste en face.	The bus stop is just across the street.
Les bus ne sont pas très fréquents.	The buses are not very frequent.
Ils passent toutes les deux heures.	They pass every two hours.
Vous pouvez y aller	You can get there
par le train/en autobus	by train/by bus
par le métro/par avion	by subway/by plane
en taxi/en auto	by taxi/by car
à bicyclette/en vélo	on a bike
Je vais à pied.	I'm going on foot.

USEFUL WORDS AND PHRASES (Dialogue 1)

tout l'après-midi	all afternoon
bien sûr	of course
rencontrer	to meet
L'Exposition ouvre	the exhibition opens
Nous devons rencontrer des collègues.	We have to meet some colleagues.
rejoindre	to meet up with
dans ce ca-là	in that case
je vous laisse	I'll leave you
les grands magasins	department stores
Je cherche de nouvelles chaussures.	I'm looking for some new shoes.
il faut en profiter	we must take advantage of it
Alors, chérie	Well, my love
n'oublie pas d'acheter des cadeaux	don't forget to buy some presents
pour les enfants	for the children

USEFUL WORDS AND PHRASES (Dialogue 2)

trop difficile	too difficult
Tu viens avec moi?	Are you coming with me?
Allons demander à Papa . . .	Let's ask Dad . . .
. . . de nous y emmener	. . . to take us there
Comme tu es paresseux!	You're so lazy!

23

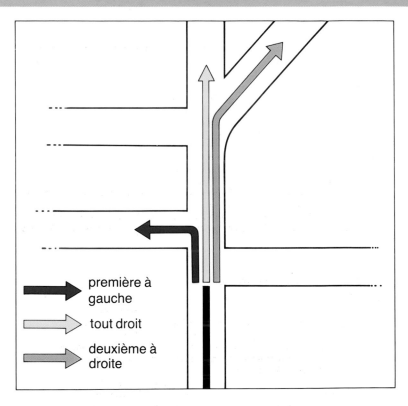

première à
gauche

tout droit

deuxième à
droite

the way it works

De *(= of)*

The word for "of" in French is **de**. I is used like this:
la valise **de** Claire (Claire's suitcase).
Use **du** before a masculine noun:
le plan **du** Métro (the map of the metro).
Use **de la** before a feminine noun:
la voiture **de la** dame (the lady's car).
Use **de l'** before a word beginning with a vowel or **h**:
le prix **de l'**emplacement (the price of the site).
Use **des** before a plural noun:
le départ **des** trains (the departure of the trains).
la chambre **des** touristes (the visitors' room).

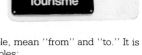

Office
de
Tourisme

Note: **de** also has other functions. It can, for example, mean "from" and "to." It is often used as a link-word, as in the following examples:
à côté **de** (beside, next to): à côté **du** restaurant
près **de** (near): près **de la** mer
en face **de** (across from): en face **de l'**hôtel

Adjectives

Most adjectives in French come after the noun: un yaourt **nature**, un café **noir**. However, some very common ones come before the noun. Here are some common adjectives which have unusual endings:

beau/belle fine, lovely, beautiful etc.

le **beau** garçon	le **bel** homme	la **belle** chambre
les **beaux** chiens		les **belles** photos

nouveau/nouvelle new

le **nouveau** sac	le **nouvel** ami	la **nouvelle** valise
les **nouveaux** projets		les **nouvelles** chaussures

vieux/vieille old

le **vieux** château	le **vieil** hôtel	la **vieille** femme
les **vieux** jardins		les **vieilles** tentes

Adjectives mostly take an **s** in the plural: les petit**s** garçons. If the noun is feminine they mostly take **es**: les grand**es** maisons.

Notice that when you want to say "some," with many adjectives (particularly feminine ones) which precede the noun, you sometimes use **de** instead of **des**: de nouvelles chaussures.

How to use the verb **aller** (to go)

Note the following phrases from the dialogues:

Pour **aller** à l'Exposition?	To get to the Exhibition?
Vous allez passer tout l'après-midi . . .?	Will you spend all afternoon . . .?
Je vais à pied.	I'm going on foot.

These are examples of the verb **aller** (to go) which is also used as a way of expressing the simple future tense, as in English (**Je vais** rejoindre une amie = *I'm going* to meet a friend). Here is the present tense:

je **vais**	I go	nous **allons**	we go
tu **vas**	you go	vous **allez**	you go
il/elle **va**	he/she/it goes	ils/elles **vont**	they go

How do I get to . . .?

There are several ways of asking for directions in French. Here are some of them.

Où est la poste, s'il vous plaît?	Where is the post office, please?
Est-ce qu'il y a une boulangerie **près d'ici**?	Is there a bakery near here?
Pour aller à la plage, s'il vous plaît?	How do I get to the beach?

or simply

S'il vous plaît, monsieur, l'Hôtel de la Plage?	The Beach Hotel, please?

things to do

2.5 You want to go to the following places. Find different ways of asking for directions.

(a) train station
(b) park
(c) restaurant
(d) Harbor Street
(e) post office (la poste)
(f) metro
(g) beach
(h) hotel
(i) bus stop
(j) bakery (la boulangerie)

2.6 Marie-Françoise is at the bus stop shown on the map and various passersby ask her for directions. Can you figure out from her instructions where it is that each of them wants to go to?

1 Continuez tout droit dans la rue Principale, et prenez la première à gauche. Puis, c'est la deuxième à gauche, et c'est sur votre droite.

2 Vous tournez à gauche dans la rue du Roi et vous prenez la première à droite. C'est à deux cents mètres, au coin de la rue.

3 C'est à côté de la mairie, juste en face du commissariat. Vous avez deux minutes à pied!

4 Longez la rue Principale, prenez la deuxième à gauche, et c'est le grand bâtiment (building) à gauche.

5 Continuez tout droit, puis c'est la deuxième rue à droite. C'est au coin, en face du petit café.

6 Tournez dans la rue du Roi et prenez la deuxième rue à gauche. Traversez la place et montez la côte. C'est juste en face, à côté du restaurant.

l'arrêt d'autobus *bus stop*	la colline *hill*	le magasin *shop*	le stade *stadium*
la banque *bank*	le commissariat de police *police station*	la mairie *town hall*	le supermarché *supermarket*
la bibliothèque *library*	l'école *school*	le musée *museum*	le syndicat d'initiative *tourist information office*
la cabine téléphonique *phone booth*	l'église *church*	le parc *park*	
le cinéma *movie theater*	les feux *traffic lights*	la piscine *swimming pool*	le théâtre *theater*
le cirque *circus*	la gare *station*	la place *square*	
	l'hôpital *hospital*	la poste *post office*	
	l'hôtel de ville *town hall*	le restaurant *restaurant*	

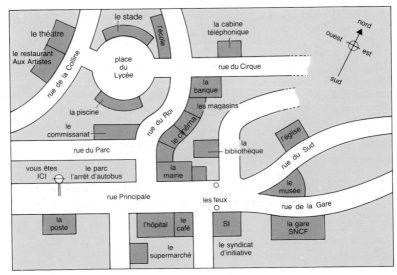

SHOPPING FOR CLOTHES, ETC.
Sizes, colors, materials

Shopping   Normal shopping hours are between 9 a.m. and about 6:30–7:30 p.m. Department stores are open all day but smaller shops often close for lunch between noon and 2 p.m. Many shops are closed on Mondays either for all or part of the day, but some food stores, particularly bakeries, are open on Sunday mornings. Supermarkets are sometimes open till 9 or 10 p.m.

aux grands magasins/at the department store

Martine goes to a department store to look for a skirt.

Vendeuse:	Vous désirez, madame?
Martine:	**Je voudrais une jupe** . . . Ah! **Cette jupe bleue est jolie, mais elle est trop grande,** je pense . . . **Avez-vous la taille au-dessous?**
Vendeuse:	Quelle taille faites-vous, madame?
Martine:	**Du quarante.**

Vendeuse:	Attendez, je vais voir . . . Non, je regrette . . . Mais cette jupe verte est jolie aussi, madame, et la noire fait très chic. La couleur est très à la mode cette année.
Martine:	Oui, c'est vrai. **Je préfère la noire. Vous avez la taille quarante en noir?**
Vendeuse:	Oui, madame, la voici. Vous voulez l'essayer?
(Martine tries it on)	
Vendeuse:	Ça fait très élègant, madame.
Martine:	Oui, **elle me plaît. Je la prends.**

Buying clothes

Vous désirez . . .?	What would you like?
Je voudrais une jupe.	I want a skirt.
Cette jupe bleue est jolie.	This blue skirt is pretty.
Elle est trop grande.	It is too big.
Il est trop grand/petit/long/court.	It is too big/small/long/short.
Avez-vous la taille au-dessous?/au-dessus?	Have you got a size smaller?/bigger?
Avez-vous quelque chose de plus petit?/de plus grand?/de moins cher?	Have you anything smaller?/bigger?/cheaper?
Quelle taille faites-vous?	What is your size?
Du quarante.	(I wear a) 40. (*see sizes chart*)
Ça fait très chic/très élégant.	It's very chic/elegant.
La couleur est très à la mode.	The color is very fashionable.
Je préfère la noire.	I prefer the black one.
Vous avez la taille quarante?	Do you have a size 40?
en noir	in black
Vous voulez l'essayer?	Do you want to try it on?
Je peux l'essayer?	Can I try it on?
Le style vous va bien.	The style suits you.
Il ne me va pas.	It doesn't suit me.
Je prendrais plutôt . . .	I'd rather have . . .
C'est vraiment difficile de choisir!	It is so difficult to choose!
Quelle couleur désirez-vous?	What color would you like?
Pouvez-vous me montrer une autre couleur?	Can you show me another color?
Attendez, je vais voir.	Wait, I'll go and see.
Non, je regrette . . .	No, I'm sorry . . .
Il/Elle coûte combien?	How much is it?
Il/Elle me plaît.	I like it.
Je le/la prends.	I'll take it.
C'est trop cher.	It's too expensive.
bon marché	cheap
Pouvez-vous l'emballer?	Could you wrap it?

Shoes

Quelle pointure faites-vous?	What shoe size are you?
(Je fais du) trente-huit.	I'm a 38. (*see sizes chart*)
une paire de chaussures	a pair of shoes
Elles sont très confortables.	They are very comfortable.
Elles me plaisent	I like them.
les sandales (f)	sandals

Clothes sizes—women

U.S.	4	6	8	10	12	14	16	
French	38	40	42	44	46	48	50	

Collar sizes—men (approximate)

U.S.	14	14½	15	15½	16	16½	17	
French	36	37	38	39/40	41	42	43	

Shoe sizes

U.S.	5	6	7	8	9	10	11	12	13	14
French	35	36	37	38	39	40	41	42	43	44

Some common shops

la papeterie	stationery store
la pharmacie	pharmacy
le magasin de chaussures	shoe store
la librairie	bookstore
le marchand de journaux	newsstand
la quincaillerie	hardware store
la droguerie	household, hardware store
le coiffeur	hair salon
le bureau de tabac	tobacco store
la bijouterie	jewelry store

au magasin de camping/at the camping shop

Henri needs a propane gas cylinder and has also forgotten to bring some essential camping items:

Vendeur: Vous désirez, monsieur?
Henri: **Je vourdrais une bouteille de camping gaz**, s'il vous plaît.
Vendeur: Oui, monsieur. Voilà. Vous désirez autre chose?
Henri: **J'ai besoin d'un tire-bouchon** . . . et aussi d'un ouvre-boîte.
Vendeur: Un ouvre-boîte comment? Montrez-moi.
Henri: (Points to a shelf) Comme ça.
Vendeur: C'est tout? Alors, ça fait quarante-cinq francs, monsieur.

At the camping supply store

une bouteille de camping gaz	a cylinder of propane gas
Vous désirez autre chose?	Anything else?
J'ai besoin de	I need
un tire-bouchon	a corkscrew
un ouvre-boît	a can opener
. . . comment?	. . . what kind?
montrez-moi	show me
comme ça	like that

Colors

clair	light	**jaune**	yellow
foncé	dark	**marron**	chestnut brown
blanc(he)	white	**pourpre**	purple
bleu	blue	**rose**	pink
brun	brown	**rouge**	red
gris	gray	**vert**	green

the way it works

More useful verbs

We have already seen **trouver** (to find) and looked at its pattern of endings (p. 10). There are many French verbs with this pattern and they are often referred to as **-er** verbs, because of the ending of the infinitive. There are two other main categories of French verbs: **-ir** and **-re**. Here is an example of each pattern:
choisir *to choose*

je chois**is**	I choose	nous chois**issons**	we choose
tu chois**is**	you choose	vous chois**issez**	you choose
il/elle chois**it**	he/she chooses	ils/elles chois**issent**	they choose

vendre *to sell*

je vend**s**	I sell	nous vend**ons**	we sell
tu vend**s**	you sell	vous vend**ez**	you sell
il/elle vend	he/she/sells	ils/elles vend**ent**	they sell

However, there are many verbs which do not exactly follow these patterns. Here are two such irregular verbs:

partir *to leave, go*

Je par**s**	I leave	nous part**ons**	we leave
tu par**s**	you leave	vous part**ez**	you leave
il/elle part	he/she/it leaves	ils/elles part**ent**	they leave

prendre *to take, have*

je prend**s**	I take	nous pren**ons**	we take
tu prend**s**	you take	vous pren**ez**	you take
il/elle prend	he/she/it takes	ils/elles pren**nent**	they take

How to say It or Them, etc. (object pronouns)

When you are talking about something that is the *object* of the sentence, use **me, te, le, la, les** instead of **je, tu, il, elle, ils, elles**, e.g.:
Je prends le gilet: Je **le** prends—I'll take *it*.
Je prends la jupe: Je **la** prends
Je préfère les pullovers: je **les** préfère—I prefer *them*.

Before a verb beginning with a vowel, use **l'** instead of **le** or **la**:
J'aime la jupe: je **l'**aime—I like *it*.

In a negative sentence, you say: Je **ne** le prends **pas**—I won't take it.

When used as object pronouns, **nous** and **vous** remain the same.

things to do

.1 Whether you want luxury goods, camping and sports equipment, or anything else, you need to know where to buy them. Do you know where the following items can be bought? Match the item to the shop.

1	une pile (battery)	**(a)**	le magasin de pêche
2	un dictionnaire (dictionary)	**(b)**	le magasin de camping
3	un filet de pêche (fishing net)	**(c)**	la librairie
4	une bouteille de parfum Dior	**(d)**	le bureau de tabac
5	des cigarettes	**(e)**	la parfumerie
6	un bracelet	**(f)**	la quincaillerie
7	un tournevis (screwdriver)	**(g)**	la droguerie
8	une poêle (frying pan)	**(h)**	la bijouterie

Now practice asking for these items: e.g.,
Bonjour, monsieur, je voudrais une pile, s'il vous plaît. Ça fait combien?

.2 You have seen a jacket that you like and you are trying it on. But somehow it isn't quite right . . .
Vendeur: Vous aimez ce blouson, monsieur?
You: [Say you don't like the color. Ask if he can show you another color, perhaps gray or brown.]

Vendeur:	Oui, monsieur. Attendez, s'il vous plaît.
You:	[Say this jacket is too big and ask if they have anything smaller.]
Vendeur:	Attendez, je vais voir. . . Oui, en voici un. Vous voulez l'essayer?
You:	[Yes, please.] . . .[Say it suits you and ask how much it is.]
Vendeur:	C'est 1000 francs.
You:	[Say you'll take it.]

3.3 After trying on some clothes you are disappointed to find that none of them fit you. Can you tell the sales clerk what's wrong?

Vendeuse:	Vous aimez cette jupe? (too small)
You:	Non, elle est trop . . .

Vendeuse:	Vous aimez cette robe?
You:	. . . .

Vendeuse:	Vous aimez ce pantalon?
You:	. . . .

Vendeuse:	Vous aimez ce jean?
You:	. . . .

Vendeuse:	Vous aimez ces chaussures?
You:	. . . .

3.4 Can you match the two halves of these statements?

1 Ces chaussures son très confortables.	**(a)** Moi aussi, alors je le prends.
2 Cette cravate en soie fait très chic.	**(b)** Oui, je les préfère.
3 Vous préférez ces gants, madame?	**(c)** Je peux l'essayer?
4 Moi, je préfère ce chapeau noir.	**(d)** Je la prends.
5 Ce manteau est beau.	**(e)** Elles me plaisent.

SHOPPING FOR FOOD

au supermarché/at the supermarket

Agathe sends Julien and Claire to the store to buy food for the picnic.

Julien: Qu'est-ce qu'il nous faut? (looks at the shopping list) . . Bon, Claire, prends un chariot.

They go around the store putting goods in the shopping cart. At the *Viandes froides* counter they ask the attendant to help them.

Julien: **Donnez-moi** deux grandes tranches de pâté de campagne, s'il vous plaît. **Je voudrais aussi deux cent cinquante grammes de** jambon . . . et **cinq cents grammes de** saucisson. Merci.

Claire: (looking in the cart) Bon, nous avons le pâté, le jambon et le saucisson, le fromage, **une plaquette de** beurre, **une boîte de** thon, **une douzaine d'**œufs . . .

Julien: Où sont les fruits? Ah, les voici.

Claire: Regarde ces belles pêches! Et j'adore les cerises . . . Achetons **un kilo de** ces jolies cerises, Julien. C'est parfait pour un picnic.

Julien: D'accord. Vraiment Claire, tu es très gourmande aujourd'hui.

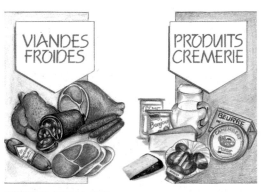

USEFUL PHRASES

Qu'est-ce qu'il nous faut?	What do we need?
Prends un chariot.	Take a shopping cart.
C'est parfait pour un picnic.	It's perfect for a picnic.
tu es très gourmande	you are very greedy

At the supermarket

Donnez-moi . . .	Give me . . .
deux grandes tranches de . . .	two big slices of . . .
pâté de campagne	coarse paté
Je voudrais aussi . . .	I also want . . .
cinq cents grammes (un demi-kilo) de . . .	500 grams (half a kilo) of . . .
deux cent cinquante grammes de . . .	250 grams of . . .
cent grammes de . . .	100 grams of . . .
un morceau de . . .	a piece of . . .
une plaquette de beurre	a slab of butter
une boîte de thon	a can of tuna
une douzaine d'œufs	a dozen eggs
Où sont les fruits?	Where is the fruit?
Regarde ces belles pêches!	Look at those lovely peaches!
J'adore les cerises.	I love cherries.
Achetons . . .	Let's buy . . .
un kilo de . . .	a kilo of . . .

Le pâté – paté
Le fromage – cheese
Le beurre – butter
Le saucisson – sausage
Le thon – tuna
Les oeufs – eggs
Le jambon – ham

Names of some common food stores

l'alimentation	food store	le marchand de	produce store
le supermarché	supermarket	légumes	
la boulangerie	bakery	le marché	market
la pâtisserie	pastry shop	la crémerie	dairy
la confiserie	candy store	la poissonnerie	fish market
la boucherie	butcher shop	libre service	self-service
la charcuterie	delicatessen	entrée libre	no obligation to buy
l'épicerie	grocery store		

Health foods

alimentation naturelle	health foods	le germe du blé	wheat germ
les produits naturels	natural products	de culture biologique	organically grown
la farine intégrale	whole wheat flour	à base de plantes	plant-based

EATING OUT

▶▶▶ **Restaurants**   There are many different categories of restaurants, ranging from those with several stars or forks offering a **menu gastronomique** to the modest **Routier**, which can serve some very good, simple food.

Before going into a restaurant, check the menus and prices that are displayed outside. Most offer one or more set menus which are often a good value. Look out for **le plat du jour** (today's special), and scan the set menu (**le menu**). There is usually a cover charge for each person (**le couvert**). Service of some 15% is often included in the bill (**service compris**), in which case it is up to you to choose whether to leave anything extra for a particularly good meal.

au restaurant/at the restaurant

Bernard, Martine, Patrick, and Sylvie arrive at the Restaurant du Gourmet.

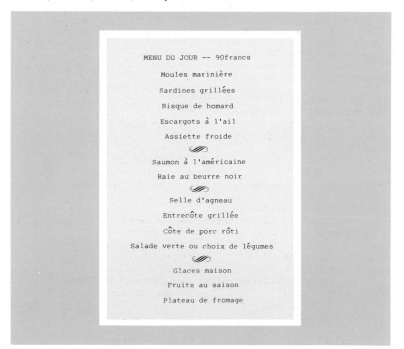

```
MENU DU JOUR -- 90francs

        Moules marinière

        Sardines grillées

        Bisque de homard

        Escargots à l'ail

        Assiette froide
              ∽

      Saumon à l'américaine

      Raie au beurre noir
              ∽

        Selle d'agneau

       Entrecôte grillée

       Côte de porc rôti

  Salade verte ou choix de légumes
              ∽

        Glaces maison

       Fruits au saison

      Plateau de fromage
```

Martine:	**Vous avez une table pour quartre personnes?**
Garçon:	Oui, messieurs-dames. Par ici, s'il vous plaît.
	(They sit down at a table)

Garçon:	Voici la carte et la carte des vins. Je vous recommande le caneton aux pruneaux qui est notre spécialité d'aujourd'hui.
Bernard:	**On va prendre le menu du jour.** Qu'est-ce que tu prends, Sylvie?
Sylvie:	**Je prends les escargots, et après la selle d'agneau.**
Martine:	Je n'ai pas grand'faim aujourd'hui. **Apportez-moi du saumon, s'il vous plaît.**
Patrick:	**Et pour moi** des moules et du caneton.
Bernard:	**Donnez-mois** des sardines et une entrecôte, s'il vous plaît.
Garçon:	Oui, monsieur. Bleu, saignant, à point?
Bernard:	Saignant.
Garçon:	Très bien, monsieur, et comme boisson?
Bernard:	**Une bouteille de vin rouge** et une bouteille de vin blanc de la maison, s'il vous plaît.

Eating out

What the waiter might say

Vous êtes combien de personnes?	How many are you?
Par ici, s'il vous plaît.	This way, please.
Voici la carte et la carte des vins.	Here is the menu and the wine list.
Je vous recommande . . .	I recommend . . .
notre spécialité d'aujourd'hui	our speciality today
Et comme boisson?	What will you have to drink?
Le service est (non) compris.	Service is (is not) included.

What you might want to say

Pouvez-vous me recommander un bon restaurant?	Can you recommend a good restaurant?
Vous avez une table . . .?	Do you have a table . . .?
pour quatre personnes	for four people
Puis-je avoir la carte?	Could I have the menu?
le menu à prix fixe/touristique	fixed-price menu/tourist menu
la carte, la carte des vins	the menu, the wine list
On va prendre le menu du jour/le menu à 90 francs.	We'll have the set meal of the day/ the 90-franc meal.
Qu'est-ce que tu prends?	What would you like?
Je prends les escargots.	I'll have the snails.
et après la selle d'agneau	and then the saddle of lamb
Je n'ai pas grand'faim.	I'm not very hungry.
Apportez-mois du saumon.	Bring me some salmon.
Et pour moi des moules et du caneton.	And for me the mussels and duck.

Donnez-moi des sardines et une entrecôte.	Give me some sardines and a steak.
bleu/saignant/à point/bien cuit	very rare/rare/medium/well done (steak)
Une bouteille de vin rouge/vin blanc	a bottle of red/white wine
de la maison	of the house
une carafe d'eau	a pitcher of water
Apportez-nous . . .	Bring us . . .
Donnez-moi . . .	Give me . . .
en supplément/en sus	extra
L'addition, s'il vous plaît.	The bill, please.
Où sont les toilettes?	Where are the toilets?

Puis-je avoir un couteau? (Could I have a knife?)

the way it works

On va prendre le menu du jour

The word **on** is used a great deal in French and can mean "one," "you," "we," "they," "people," etc.

On dit que . . .	They (people) say that . . .
Est-ce-qu'**on** peut stationner ici?	Can one (we) park here?
Qu'est-ce qu'**on** mange?	What shall we eat?

Telling someone what to do

When you are telling or ordering someone to do something, or merely making a suggestion, you use a form of the verb called the imperative. It works like this:

regard**e** ces pêches	look at these peaches (to a child, or someone you know well)
regard**ez** la liste	look at the list (to someone you don't know very well or more than one person)
regard**ons** l'horaire	let's look at the schedule

There are many examples of verbs in the imperative in this book. Here are just a few of them:

N'oubli**ez** pas (don't forget)   attend**ez** (wait)   pren**ez** (take)   pren**ons** (let's take)

things to do

3.5 Vous faites des courses! You are going shopping!

Here are some useful phrases when buying food.

Weights and measures

un kilo de	a kilo of
un demi-kilo de	half a kilo of
une livre de	a pound of
cent grammes de	100 grams of
un litre de	a liter of
un demi-litre de	half a liter of

Useful adjectives

râpé/moulu	grated/ground
en poudre	granulated

Containers and quantities

une boîte de	a can/a box of
un paquet de	a pack of
une barquette de	a carton of
un morceau de	a piece of
une tranche de	a slice of
une plaquette de	a slab of (butter)
une douzaine de	a dozen
un peu (de)	a little (of)
beaucoup (de)	a lot (of)

Here is your shopping-list.

250 grammes de beurre
1 morceau de fromage
½ kilo de sucre en poudre
1 litre de lait
200 grammes de pâté de campagne
4 tranches de jambon
1 boîte de soupe de poisson
1 kilo de pommes
1 livre de poires
½ litre de vinaigre
100 grammes de salade russe
1 barquette de carottes rapées
1 paquet de café moulu
2 bouteilles de vin rouge
1 douzaine d'oeufs

Practice asking for each item in turn, e.g., Je voudrais deux cent cinquante grammes de beurre.

Now say what the list would be in English.

3.6 You are in a bakery (see p. 82).

Ask for the items shown.
Ask how much it all comes to.

3.7 You are at a restaurant with a party of friends. Tell the waiter in French what everyone would like to eat or drink.

Oysters, then steak and **fries** and a glass of red wine.

Seafood, chicken, and white wine — and no potatoes.

Frog's legs, pork, and a glass of beer please. And a green salad with the pork.

Apple **pie** and ice cream for me, and a cda.

broth then trout, and a bottle of mineral water for me please.

fries and an orange juice.

3.8 You could go to a café where the following conversation might take place:

Garçon: Bonjour, vous désirez?
You: **Je prends un sandwich au fromage**, s'il vous plaît.
Garçon: Très bien, et comme boisson?
You: **Un verre de cola.**
Garçon: Voilà, monsieur/mademoiselle.
You: **Merci. L'addition, s'il vous plaît.**

Here is a list of the kinds of food and drink you might want:

un casse-croûte	snack	**une omelette au fromage**	cheese omelette
un sandwich au jambon	ham sandwich	**des frites**	french fries
un américain	ham salad sandwich	**une gaufre**	waffle
		un hamburger	hamburger
un sandwich au fromage	cheese sandwich	**un hot dog**	hot dog
		des brochettes	kebabs
un croque-monsieur	grilled cheese and ham sandwich	**une glace**	ice cream
		une crêpe	pancake

And you might like one of the following to drink:

une jus de tomates	tomato juice	**un verre de cidre**	cider
un jus de pommes	apple juice	**une (bière) blonde**	lager
un citron pressé	lemonade	**une pression**	draft beer
une limonade	soda	**un panaché**	beer mixed with soda
un thé au lait/ nature/au citron	tea with milk/plain/ with lemon	**un café noir/ crème**	black coffee/coffee with milk
		une express	espresso
un chocolat chaud	hot chocolate	**un lait frappé**	milk shake
un cola	cola		

Now try to make up conversations of your own!

BANK, POST OFFICE, TELEPHONE

Banks and paying Banks are open from approximately 9 to 12 and 2 to 4, except in larger towns, where they may not close for lunch. They are closed either all day Monday, or on Saturday afternoons. Banks close early the day before public holidays in France. **Bureaux de change** (currency exchange offices) are open longer hours, though rates of exchange may alter outside normal banking hours.

ATMs are a convenient way to withdraw money while traveling in France. ATMs are prevalent in large cities such as Paris, as well as smaller towns throughout the country. Credit cards are also widely accepted.

à la banque/at the bank

Claire and Julien want to hire a windsurfer (**une planche à voile**), but first Claire needs to go to the bank to change some checks.

Employé: Bonjour, mademoiselle.

Claire: Bonjour, monsieur. **Puis-je changer de l'argent?**

Employé: Oui, mademoiselle. Vous avez des chèques de voyage?

Claire: Oui, **Je veux encaisser ces deux chèques** de dix livres.

Employé: Alors, signez ici, et donnez-moi votre passeport. Vingt livres, ça fait . . . (fills in form and calculates amount) Alors, voilà votre passeport, et maintenant, passez à la caisse.

Julien: Montre-moi ton passeport, Claire. Oh, quelle jolie photo!

Claire: Ne sois pas idiot—la photo est affreuse!

(They go to the cashier.)

Caissier: Voilà, mademoiselle. Un billet de cent francs, deux billets de cinquante, et deux pièces de dix francs.

Julien: Très bien. (to Claire) Allons à la plage.

At the bank/at the currency exchange (au bureau de change)

Je veux/voudrais . . .	I would like to . . .
Puis-je/Est-ce que je peux . . .?	Can I . . .?
changer de l'argent	change some money
changer vingt dollars	change twenty dollars
encaisser ces chèques de voyage/	change these traveler's checks
ces chèques travellers	
J'ai une carte bancaire.	I have a bank card.
une carte de crédit	a credit card
un carnet de chèques	a checkbook
une lettre de crédit	a letter of credit
Quel est le taux de change aujourd'hui?	What is the exchange rate today?
Voici un billet de cent francs.	Here is a hundred-franc bill.
une pièce de dix francs	a ten-franc coin
cinquante centimes	fifty centimes
de la monnaie	some change
Voulez-vous remplir cette fiche/formulaire?	Would you fill out this form?
Signez ici.	Sign here.
Ça fait . . .	That comes to . . .
Passez à la caisse.	Go to the cashier.

USEFUL WORDS AND PHRASES

Montre-moi ton passeport.	Show me your passport.
Quelle jolie photo!	What a lovely photo!
Ne sois pas idiot.	Don't be stupid.
Elle est affreuse.	It's awful.

Post offices and stamps   The post office (**Postes et Télécommunications —P&T/PTT**) is open from 8 a.m. to 7 p.m. Monday through Friday and from 8 a.m. to noon on Saturdays. Mailboxes in France and Switzerland are yellow, and have different slots for local and out-of-town mail. In Belgium, mailboxes are red. You can arrange to receive letters from the *Poste Restante* (general delivery) counter at central post offices, and these can be picked up for a small fee and upon production of your passport.

In France, stamps can be bought at a **bureau de tabac** (recognizable by its distinctive red cone sign), from some cafés, or from the post office.

au bureau de tabac/at the tobacconist's

Patrick and Bernard go to a *tabac* to buy some stamps and stop to look at the postcard stand outside.

Patrick: Il me faut cinq cartes postales. Ah, cette vue de la Seine est assez belle. Mais, qu'est-ce que c'est, Bernard?

Bernard: Ça, c'est le Centre Georges Pompidou.

Patrick: Ah bon? Je prends celle-là aussi. (He goes to the counter.) **Vous avez des timbres**, monsieur?

Marchand: C'est pour quelle destination, monsieur?

Patrick: **C'est pour l'Angleterre**—et je veux aussi un timbre pour les Etats-Unis.

Marchand: J'ai des timbres pour la Grande Bretagne, mais je n'ai pas de timbres pour les Etats-Unis. Il faut aller à la poste, à côté.

Patrick: Alors, **donnez-moi quartre timbres pour des cartes postales et un pour une lettre**, pour l'Angleterre. **Est-ce que vous vendez des journaux aussi?**

Marchand: Non, monsieur. Le kiosque à journaux est en face.

(At the newsstand)

Marchand: Un journal irlandais? Je regrette, monsieur, je n'ai pas de journaux irlandais—mais j'ai un journal anglais. Le voici.

Patrick: *The Independent*? Bon, je le prends.

At the tabac/at the post office

Il me faut cinq carte postales.	I need five postcards.
Vous avez des timbres/un carnet de timbres?	Do you have any stamps?/a book of stamps?
C'est pour quelle destination?	Where is it for?
C'est pour l'Angleterre/la Grande Bretagne/les Etats-Unis.	It's for England/Great Britain/the USA.
Donnez-moi un timbre pour une lettre/pour une carte postale.	Give me a stamp for a letter/for a postcard.
La poste/le bureau de poste est à côté.	The post office is next door.
Je voudrais envoyer cette lettre/ce paquet/ce colis.	I would like to send this letter/this packet/this parcel.
. . . par avion/express/en recommande/ avec accusé de réception	. . . by airmail/express/registered/with recorded delivery
Où est la boîte aux lettres?	Where is the mailbox?
Où se trouve le guichet de poste restante?	Where is the general delivery counter?
Y a-t-il du courrier pour moi?	Is there any mail for me?

At the newsstand

Le kiosque à journaux est en face.	The newsstand is across the street.
Vous avez des journaux américains?	Do you have any American newspapers?
Je n'ai pas de journaux irlandais.	I don't have any Irish newspapers.
J'ai un journal anglais.	I have an English newspaper.

USEFUL WORDS AND PHRASES

Cette vue est assez belle.	That view is rather pretty.	Ça, c'est . . .	That's . . .
		Ah bon?	Really?
Qu'est-ce que c'est?	What's that?	Je prends celle-là.	I'll take that one.

Where are you from?

Nationalities and languages/Les nationalités et les langues

Je viens de France.	I am from France.	**Je parle français.**	I speak French.
Je suis Français(e).	I am French.	**des journaux français**	French newspapers

Use a capital letter when talking about someone's nationality, and a small letter when talking about the language.

Telephones   In France, you can find public phones in post offices, Métro stations, most cafés, and on the street. Almost all phones take special phone cards (**télécartes**), which can be purchased at *tabacs*, newsstands, etc. Using a phone card is the easiest way to make calls both within France and internationally, as it's difficult to find phones that accept coins.

conversation téléphonique/telephone conversation

The Bergeron family is organizing a beach barbecue for Sunday. Claire wants to invite Cathy, an English friend who is staying with a family in a nearby town. At the camp office, she dials the number.

Mme Leverd:	**Allô? Ici le 84-58-29.**
Claire:	**Allô, je voudrais parler à** Cathy, s'il vous plaît.
Mme Leverd:	Oui. C'est de la part de qui?
Claire:	**C'est** Claire Rogers, une camarade anglaise.

Mme Leverd:	Attendez un instant. Je vais la chercher, mais je crois qu'elle est à la poste. (Shouts, "Cathy!"... Pause . . .) Non, elle n'est pas là en ce moment. Vous voulez lui laisser un message?
Claire:	Je voudrais l'inviter à un barbecue sur la plage à S. Jean-sur-Mer. C'est pour dimanche soir à dix-huit heures.
Mme Leverd:	Ah, vous êtes bien gentille. Je crois qu'elle est libre dimanche soir.
Claire:	**Pouvez-vous lui dire de me téléphoner** au camping? **C'est le numéro** 86-22-51.
Mme Leverd:	D'accord. Je vais le lui dire. Merci beaucoup, mademoiselle. Au revoir.
Claire:	Au revoir, madame.

Using the telephone

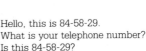

Allô, ici le 84-58-29.	Hello, this is 84-58-29.
Quel est votre numéro de téléphone?	What is your telephone number?
C'est bien le 84-58-29?	Is this 84-58-29?
Vous avez fait un mauvais numéro.	
Vous vous êtes trompé de numéro.	You've got the wrong number.
Vous faites erreur.	
Je voudrais parler à . . .	I'd like to speak to . . .
Vous pouvez me passer le poste 18?	Give me extension 18.
C'est de la part de qui?	Who's speaking?
Qui est à l'appareil?	Who is it?
Attendez un instant.	Wait a moment.
Je vais le/la chercher.	I'll go and look for him/her.
C'est lui-/elle-même à l'appareil.	Yes, speaking.
Ne quittez pas (*operator*).	Hold the line, please.

Elle n'est pas là en ce moment.	She's not here at the moment.
Vous voulez lui laisser un message?	Do you want to leave her a message?
Pouvez-vous lui dire de me téléphoner?	Could you ask he to phone me?
Je vais le lui dire.	I'll tell her.
Vous voulez rappeler plus tard?	Do you want to call back later?
Vous pouvez répéter, s'il vous plaît?	Could you repeat that, please?
la cabine téléphonique	phone booth
téléphoner par l'automatique	to dial direct
composer le numéro	to dial the number
attendre la tonalité	to wait for the dial tone
une communication personelle	personal call
en PVC	collect call
le/la standardiste	operator
l'annuaire	directory
un jeton	token
des pièces de 5F, 1F, ½ F	5-franc/1 franc/½ franc coins
l'indicatif du département	area code

USEFUL WORDS AND PHRASES

la camarade	friend	**Je crois que . . .**	I think that . . .
gentil(le)	nice, kind	**elle est libre**	she's free

the way it works

Who? and What?

Who? is **Qui est-ce qui?** or **Qui?**:

Qui est-ce qui parle anglais?	Who speaks English?
Qui est à l'appareil?	Who is speaking? (on telephone)

What? is **Qu'est-ce que?** or **Que?**:

Qu'est-ce que vous faites?	What are you doing?
Que cherchez-vous?	What are you looking for?

If you want to know what something is you use **Qu'est-ce que c'est?**:

Qu'est-ce que c'est? C'est la Tour Eiffel.	What is it? It's the Eiffel Tower.
Qu'est-ce que c'est? C'est un hélicoptère.	What is it? It's a helicopter.

Which? and What?

To ask "which?" you use **Quel** before a masculine noun (**Quel** timbre? Which stamp?) and **Quelle** before a feminine noun (**Quelle** destination?).
Here are two more examples:

Quel est le taux de change?	What is the exchange rate?
Quelle est la date aujourd'hui?	What is the date today?

The words **Quel** and **Quelle** are also used in exclamations:

Quel beau temps!	What beautiful weather!
Quelle jolie photo!	What a lovely photo!

For words in the plural, use **Quels** and **Quelles**.

This One and That One

You know how to say "this" or "that" (**ce** timbre—this stamp; **cette** carte postale—that post card). However, if you want to distinguish between "this one" and "that one," you can do it like this:

masculine		*feminine*	
celui-ci	this one	**celle-ci**	this one
celui-là	that one	**celle-là**	that one
ceux-ci	these ones	**celles-ci**	these ones
ceux-là	those ones	**celles-là**	those ones

Ceci and **cela** refer to "this" or "that" in a general way. **Cela** is usually shortened to **ça**, and this is used a lot.

Ça fait trente francs.	That comes to 30F.
Ça c'est le Centre Georges Pompidou.	That's the Pompidou Center.

All and everything

The word for "all" is **tout** (**tous** = plural) with a masculine noun and **toute** (**toutes** = plural) with a feminine noun. The word **tout** on its own means "everything."

Here are some common expressions using **tout/toute**:

tout le monde	everybody
tout le temps	all the time
toute la famille	all the family
toute la soirée	all evening
tous les jours	every day (**toujours** = always)
tous les deux	both (masc.)
toutes les jeunes filles	all the girls

How to say you don't have any

J'ai means "I have": J'ai du fromage (*I have some cheese*); J'ai des journaux (*I have some newspapers*).

To say "I don't have" you use "**Je n'ai pas**": Je n'ai pas de fromage; Je n'ai pas de journaux.

Note that if the verb is negative you use the word **de** for "any" (not **des**).

Expressions with *avoir*

J'ai is a form of the verb **avoir** (see Mardi p. 17 for the complete pattern). This verb can be used in a number of very common expressions meaning "I am," "you are," etc.

J'ai faim/soif.	I am hungry/thirsty.	**J'ai** horreur de . . .	I hate . . .
Tu as chaud/froid.	You are hot/cold.	**Nous avons** peur.	We are frightened.
Quel âge **avez-vous**?	How old are you?	**Vous avez** raison.	You are right.
Il a vingt ans.	He is twenty.	**Ils ont** tort.	They are wrong.

(NB If you want to say "I'm not hungry" you say: **Je n'ai pas faim**.)

Some more verbs

You know how to say "I would like" (je **voudrais**) and "Do you want?" (**voulez-vous?**). Here is the verb **vouloir** (to wish or want):

je **veux**	nous **voulons**
tu **veux**	vous **voulez**
il/elle **veut**	ils/elles **veulent**

Two other useful verbs are **venir** (to come) and **pouvoir** (to be able):

Je **viens**	nous **venons**	je **peux** (I can)	nous **pouvons**
tu **viens**	vous **venez**	tu **peux**	vous **pouvez**
il/elle **vient**	ils/elles **viennent**	il/elle **peut**	ils/elles **peuvent**

Pronouns—the indirect object

Sometimes a sentence has what is called an "indirect object." Look at this sentence from the third dialogue:

Vous voulez lui laisser un message?   Do you want to leave her a message?

In this sentence, the message is the direct object and Cathy ("her") is the indirect object.

In French, the pronouns **me, te, nous** and **vous** are used for both direct and indirect objects, but **lui** and **leur** are used for indirect objects only.
Look for the indirect object after these verbs:

parler (to speak):	Je parle à ma mère.	Je **lui** parle. (I speak to her.)
téléphoner (to phone):	Elle téléphone à ses amies.	Elle **leur** téléphone. (She phones them.)
dire (to say):	Je dis à cet enfant . . .	Je **lui** dis . . . (I say to him . . .)
donner (to give):	Je donne à ces garçons . . .	Je **leur** donne . . . (I give them . . .)
écrire (to write):	Vous écrivez à votre père.	Vous **lui** écrivez. (You write to him.)

You would also say:

Il **me** parle. (He speaks to me.)	Je **te** donne. (I give (to) you.)
Elle **nous** écrit. (She writes to us.)	Ils **vous** téléphonent. (They telephone you.)

Reflexive verbs

You may have noticed in this book some verbs which have, for example, **me, te** or **se** placed between the subject and the verb itself: je **m**'appelle, je **me** présente, etc. These are called reflexive pronouns and they can often be translated by using the words "myself," "yourself," etc.

appeler   to call   s'appeler   to be called (call oneself)

Here is the full list of reflexive pronouns:

me	myself	**nous**	ourselves
te	yourself	**vous**	yourselves
se	himself/herself/oneself	**se**	themselves

things to do

4.1 Can you match up these pairs of sentences so that they make sense?

1 Regardez les Alpes!	(a) C'est pour quelle destination?
2 Est-ce que vous avez des journaux?	(b) Quelle jolie vue!
	(c) Quels journaux voulez-vous?
3 Ah Bernard, c'est vous?	(d) Quelle marque (brand) voulez-vous?
4 Je voudrais envoyer cette lettre.	
5 Vous voulez encaisser ces chèques?	(e) Quelle surprise!
	(f) Quel est le taux de change?
6 Je voudrais des cigarettes, s'il vous plaît.	

4.2 Say what you want

In the supermarket you need various items at the delicatessen counter and it's a matter of pointing out to the attendant which cheese, etc., you want. Use celui-ci or celui-là, celle-ci or celle-là in your answer.

Assistant: Quel fromage voulez-vous, madame? Celui-ci ou celui-là?
You: [This one please.]
Assistant: Et quelle quiche voulez-vous, madame?
You: [That one, please.]
Assistant: Et quel pâté voulez-vous, madame?
You: [This one, please.]
Assistant: Quel saucisson voulez-vous, madame?
You: [This one and that one, please.] Je prends du fromage, de la quiche, du pâté et des saucissons.

4.3 You are at a post office in France. Tell the clerk what you need:

Assistant: Bonjour, monsieur/madame. Vous désirez?
Vous: [Tell him you want to buy some stamps.]
Assistant: Pour des lettres ou pour des cartes postales?
Vous: [Say you want to send one letter and two postcards.]
Assistant: Très bien. C'est pour quelle destination?
Vous: [Tell him the letter is for England, and the postcards are for the USA.]
Assistant: C'est tout?
Vous: [Say no, you want to send a package to Paris.]

4.4 You are in a bank.
1 Ask the teller what the day's exchange rate is.
2 Ask whether you can cash a check.
3 Say you want to exchange $50 worth of traveler's checks.
4 Say you want to exchange a 100-franc bill for ten 10-franc coins.

4.5 See if you can complete this telephone conversation. Look in the phrasebook section if you get stuck.

Vous:	. . . .
Mme Gérard:	Oui, c'est le 87-23-25.
Vous:	. . . .
Mme Gérard:	Vous voulez parlez à M. Lotte? C'est de la part de qui?
Vous:	. . . .
Mme Gérard:	Oh pardon—il n'est pas là en ce moment.
Vous:	[Ask if he can call you back.] . . . .
Mme Gérard:	Quel est votre numéro?
Vous:	. . . .
Mme Gérard:	Bon, je vais lui donner le message. Merci et au revoir.
Vous:	. . . .

4.6 See if you can shorten these sentences by using indirect object pronouns. The first one is done for you.
1 Claire parle à l'employé de banque.
   Claire lui parle.
2 Bernard dit bonjour à la marchande de tabac.
   Bernard . . . .
3 Le caissier donne un billet de 100F à Julien.
   Le caissier . . . .
4 Agathe téléphone à son mari.
   Elle . . . .
5 Claire écrit à ses parents en Angleterre.
   Elle . . . .

ILLNESS AND ACCIDENTS

The pharmacy   A **pharmacie** is a pharmacy, while a **droguerie** (similar to a drugstore) sells household goods and toiletries. The **pharmacie** can be recognized by its illuminated green cross in the window. You can go to the **pharmacien** for helpful medical advice as well as for first aid treatment. A schedule of local pharmacies open at night is posted in the shop.

à la pharmacie/at the pharmacy

Bernard has eaten and drunk too much at the restaurant and is paying a visit to the pharmacist.

Bernard:	**Ah, j'ai mal à la tête.**
Pharmacienne:	Vous avez de la fièvre?
Bernard:	Non, mais hier j'ai trop mangé et trop bu. **Est-ce que vous avez quelque chose contre une gueule be bois?**

| Pharmacienne: | Voyons, monsieur, vous avez sans doute une crise de foie. Je vous recommande ces comprimés que vous devez prendre trois fois par jour. Mais il faut boire seulement de l'eau pendant trois jours—vous allez vous sentir mieux bientôt. |
| Bernard: | Ah bon? Merci, je l'espère bien. |

Illness   You might wish to purchase traveler's insurance before leaving for France. Check with your insurance agent. In cases of minor injuries and illnesses, you will usually find the pharmacist is very helpful. Pharmacists may sell and recommend medicine that is often only available in the U.S. by prescription. If you take prescription medicine, always carry your prescription with you.

Un accident

Julien and Claire did not have a very successful morning's windsurfing, and Julien has hurt his leg.

Agathe:	Ah mon Dieu, qu'est-ce qui est arrivé?
Julien:	(groaning) C'est ma jambe. **J'ai mal à la jambe.**
Claire:	Oui, il est tombé dans l'eau plusieurs fois, et il s'est fait vraiment mal à la jambe. Il est très maladroit, n'est-ce pas?
Agathe:	Tu es couvert de bleus, Julien. Il faut t'emmener chez le médecin!

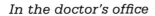

In the doctor's office

Médecin:	Alors, c'est le genou qui vous fait mal?
Julien:	**Non, docteur, c'est la cheville. Elle est toute gonflée.**
Médecin:	(examining the ankle) Ça fait mal ici?
Julien:	Aïe, ne touchez pas, je vous en prie. C'est très douloureux.
Médecin:	(tutting) A mon avis, ce n'est pas trop grave. Mais pour nous en assurer, je vais vous envoyer à l'hôpital pour passer des radios. En attendant, je vais vous panser la cheville, jeune homme.
Julien:	Oh non! Mes vacances sont gâchées!

Illnesses and injuries

Je ne me sens pas bien/Ça ne va pas bien/Je ne vais pas bien.	I don't feel well.
Je suis malade/Je suis blessé(e).	I am ill/I am hurt.
J'ai mal à/au/aux . . .	My . . . hurts.*
J'ai mal à la tête/au ventre.	I have a headache/a stomachache.
au cœur.	I feel sick.
J'ai mal partout.	I ache everywhere.
J'ai vomi.	I vomited.
J'ai une crise de foie.	I have an upset stomach.
Je tousse.	I have a cough.
J'ai un rhume.	I have a cold.
J'ai attrapé un coup de soleil.	I have a sunburn.
J'ai mal aux dents.	I have a toothache.
aux gencives	sore gums
Etes-vous blessé(e)?	Are you hurt?
Je me suis foulé le poignet.	I have sprained by wrist.
cogné la tête	banged my head
brûlé la main	burned my hand
coupé le pied	cut my foot
tordu le genou*	twisted my knee
Il s'est fait mal à la jambe.	He has hurt his leg.
Il est tombé dans l'eau.	He fell in the water.
Tu es couvert de bleus!	You're covered with bruises!
Le bras est cassé.	The (my) arm is broken.
La cheville est gonflée.	The (my) ankle is swollen.
Ne touchez pas . . . c'est douloureux!	Don't touch . . . it's painful!
Je suis allergique à la pénicilline.	I am allergic to penicillin.
Je suis cadiaque.	I have a heart condition.
Je suis asthmatique.	I am asthmatic.
Je suis diabétique.	I am diabetic.
Je suis enceinte.	I am pregnant.
Je prends la pilule.	I am on the pill.
J'ai perdu mes comprimés.	I have lost my pills.

*Note that where in English, you would say "*my* head," etc., in French you generally use **le, la** or **les** when talking about parts of the body.

Medical advice

Il faut emmener Julien chez le médicin.	We must take Julien to see the doctor.
Je voudrais un rendez-vous.	I'd like an appointment.
Vous avez l'air malade.	You look ill.
Vous avez de la fièvre?	Do you have a temperature?
C'est le genou qui vous fait mal?	Is it your knee that's hurting?
Ça fait mal ici?	Does this hurt?
Ce n'est pas trop grave.	It isn't too serious.
Ne vous inquiétez pas.	Don't worry.
Reposez-vous	Rest (yourself).
Vous devez en prendre soin.	Look after it.
Vous devez garder le lit.	You must stay in bed.
Je vais vous envoyer à l'hôpital pour passer des radios.	I'm going to send you to hospital to have an X ray.

Je vais vous panser la cheville.	I will bandage your ankle.
Il vous faut un plâtre.	You need a cast.
Je vais vous faire une piqûre.	I'm going to give you an injection.
Je vais vous faire une ordonnance.	I'm going to give you a prescription.
Je vous recommande . . .	I recommend . . .
Vous devez prendre . . .	You must take . . .
Prenez des calmants.	Take painkillers.
trois fois par jour	three times a day
Je vous conseille de	I advise you to
. . . manger très peu	. . . eat very little
. . . boire seulement de l'eau	. . . drink only water
Vous allez vous sentir mieux bientôt.	You will feel better soon.
le médecin	doctor
Les heures de consultation	Office hours
Le service d'urgence	Emergency room

J'ai trop mangé et trop bu.	I had too much to eat and drink.
Je voudrais quelque chose contre . . .	I want someting for . . .
le constipation/la diarrhée	constipation/diarrhea
la dyspépsie/la flatulence/la gueule de bois	indigestion/wind/a hangover
Je me suis fait piquer par	I have been stung by
une méduse/un oursin/	a jellyfish/a sea urchin/
un moustique/une guêpe	a mosquito/a wasp
une cuillerée à café	a spoonful
avant/après les repas	before/after meals
pendant trois jours	for three days

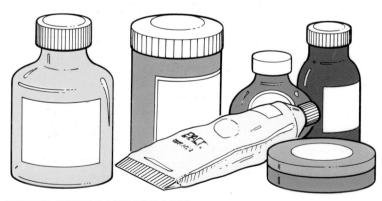

USEFUL WORDS AND PHRASES

hier	yesterday	maladroit	clumsy
voyons	let's see	je vous en prie	Please
sans doute	no doubt	à mon avis	in my opinion
que	which/that	pour nous en	to reassure
Ah bon?	Really?	assurer	ourselves
Je l'espère bien.	I hope so.	en attendant	in the meantime
Qu'est-ce qui est arrivé?	What happened?	Mes vacances sont gâchées!	My vacation is ruined!

the way it works

Devoir (must, ought to, have to)

To say "you must" do something in French you use a form of the verb **devoir** + a second verb in the infinitive:

Je dois partir tout de suite.	I must leave at once.
Vous devez garder le lit.	You must stay in bed.
Vous devez prendre les comprimés.	You must take the pills.

Here is the complete verb:

je **dois**	nous **devons**
tu **dois**	vous **devez**
il/elle **doit**	ils/elles **doivent**

What happened yesterday? (Qu'est-ce qui s'est passé hier?)

If you are talking about something that happened yesterday, you will need to use a verb in the **past tense**. In this unit you will find several examples of verbs in the past tense, e.g., Bernard **ate** and **drank** too much; Julien **fell** into the water.

The simple past tense in French uses either **avoir** or **être** and a form of the verb called the past participle. Here are some examples using **avoir**:

Le vendredi je mange de poisson.	On Fridays I eat fish.
Hier, **j'ai mangé** des moules.	Yesterday, I ate some mussels.
Je travaille chez moi tous les matins.	I work at home every morning.
La semaine dernière **j'ai travaillé** l'après-midi aussi.	Last week I worked in the afternoon too.

Many verbs in French have past participles ending in **é**. Unfortunately, however, there are a number of different past participle endings, which must be learned. Here is a list of some common verbs and their past participles:

attendre (to wait for)	**attendu**	être (to be)	**été**
avoir (to have)	**eu**	faire (to do, make)	**fait**
boire (to drink)	**bu**	finir (to finish)	**fini**
comprendre (to understand)	**compris**	lire (to read)	**lu**
dire (to say)	**dit**	prendre (to take)	**pris**
dormir (to sleep)	**dormi**	voir (to see)	**vu**

Qui and que (who, that, which)

When referring to the object of a sentence, use **que** instead of **qui**:

Le médicament **qui** est dans la bouteille verte a un très mauvais goût.	The medicine that is in the green bottle tastes very bad.
Le médicament **que** Claire a acheté est meilleur.	The medicine that Claire bought is better.

things to do

5.1 A hypochondriac is arriving at the doctor's office. Can you tell what's wrong with him? Begin: **Il a mal . . .**(See list on p. 83.)

1 2 3

4 5 6

5.2 At the pharmacy. (See list on p. 81)

1 You want to buy something to prevent sunburn. What do you ask for?
(a) la crème à raser (b) la crème solaire (c) la pellicule

2 You need a bandage for your finger. Do you ask for
(a) de la pommade (b) du tricostéril (c) du sparadrap?

3 The pharmacist gives you your mediation and tells you to take the pills twice a day after meals. Does he tell you
(a) deux fois par jour avant les repas (b) trois fois par jour après les repas (c) deux fois par jour après les repas?

4 You go to the pharmacy to buy toothpaste, soap, and razor blades. What do you ask for?
(a) du dentifrice, du savon et des lames à raser (b) une brosse à dents, du savon et des lames à raser (c) du dentifrice, du savon et de la crème à raser

BUYING GAS AND DRIVING

▷ **Driving**   An international driver's license is not necessary for driving in France if you are traveling on vacation. National car rental chains have offices in all the airports and cities, as well as in many smaller towns. Remember that in Europe, most cars have standard transmission. If you want to rent a car with automatic transmission, you must request one when you reserve in advance. It is a good idea to carry comprehensive insurance and make certain that the registration and rental contract are in the car at all times. Wearing your seatbelt is compulsory in France, and you can be pulled over for not having it on. You are not allowed to stop on an open road, unless you drive right off the road.

You must give way to the right (**priorité à droite**) in towns and cities, although elsewhere, main roads now have the right of way. You should look out for the signs: **Vous n'avez pas priorité** (You do not have right of way) and **Passage protégé** (right of way). Note that moving violations often carry on-the-spot fines.

▷ **Freeways** have phones at intervals of 2 km and all-night gas stations every 20 km. Many freeways in France have tolls (**autoroute à péage**). In Switzerland, you need to buy a sticker for your windshield before using a freeway.

French roads are designated as follows: **autoroute (A)** (freeway); **route nationale (N)** (main road); **route départementale (D)** (secondary road); **route européenne (E)** (minor road); **route forestière (RF)** (forest road).

à la station-service/at the gas station

The van carrying Patrick's display stands is on its way to Roissy. The driver stops to buy gas.

Pompiste: Bonjour, monsieur.
Conducteur: Bonjour, madame. **Trente litres d'essence, s'il vous plaît.**
Pompiste: Ordinaire ou super?
Conducteur: **Super.**
Pompiste: (fills tank) Voilà, monsieur, ça fait 115F. Merci et au revoir.

On the road French **speed limits** are as follows: 130 kmph (80 mph) on toll roads, 110 (68) on freeways and divided highways, 90 (56) on other roads and 60 (37) in town. Note that all speed limits are reduced on wet roads. Drinking and driving carries a heavy fine, and there are random breath tests. **Parking restrictions** vary from town to town, but may be on one or other side of the street at different times of the month. Most downtown areas have parking zones, and in **zone bleue** areas, parking disks (**disques de stationnement**) must be set to the time of arrival and length of stay. These can be obtained from newsstands, tourist offices and gas stations.

un accrochage/an accident

The driver turns out of the gas station into the road but doesn't see a Renault 5 that is approaching quite fast . . . The gas station attendant is the first on the scene.

Pompiste: (to driver of Renault 5) Vous êtes blessée, mademoiselle?
Conductrice: Ah, mon bras, **Je crois qu'il est cassé**.
Pompiste: (to first driver) C'est de votre faute, monsieur.
Conducteur: **Je suis vraiment désolé,** mademoiselle, je ne vous ai pas vue.
Conductrice: Qu'est-ce que j'ai mal, mon bras, mon bras!
Pompiste: Mon fils a déjà appelé une ambulance. Ne vous inquiétez pas, mademoiselle. Venez vous asseoir, reposez-vous.
Conducteur: Mon Dieu, quelle catastrophe! Je suis déjà en retard!
Pompiste: Calmez-vous, monsieur. Voici la police. Tout va s'arranger.

A la station-service (at the gas station)

30 litres d'essence, s'il vous plaît	30 litres of gas, please
50 francs, s'il vous plaît	50 francs' worth, please
Faites le plein.	Fill it up.
Ordinaire ou super?	2-star or 4-star? (regular or super)
l'essence sans plomb	unleaded gas
le gasoil	diesel
Donnez-moi de l'huile, s.v.p.	I'd like some oil, please.
Donnez-moi de l'eau.	I'd like some water.
Je voudrais vérifier la pression des pneus.	I'd like to check the tire pressure.

Au garage (at the garage)

Je suis en panne.	My car has broken down.
J'ai un pneu crevé.	I've got a flat tire.
Est-ce que vous avez un service de dépannage?	Do you have road service?
Ça ne marche pas	It's not working.
L'auto ne démarre pas.	The car won't start.

Road signs

Allumez vos phares.	Turn on your lights.
Attention travaux	Roadwork ahead
Chaussée déformée	Damaged road surface
Déviation	Detour
Interdiction de doubler	No passing
Passage à niveau	Railroad crossing
Poids lourds	Heavy loads
Ralentir	Slow down
Stationnement interdit	No parking
Sens interdit	No entry
Verglas	Icy road
Virages sur 2 km	Curves for 2 km

Accidents and emergencies

Au secours!/Vite!	Help!/Quick!
Qu'est-ce qui est arrivé?	What happened?
Il y a eu un accident/accrochage.	There's been an accident/collision.
Il y a des blessés.	Some people have been hurt.
Il faut appeler une ambulance/la police.	We must call an ambulance/the police.
le commissariat/le poste de police	police station
Il faut l'emmener à l'hôpital.	We must take him/her to the hospital.
les premiers soins	first aid
emplacements des postes de secours	location of first aid stations
la sortie de secours	emergency exit
glace à briser	break the glass
en cas d'accident	in case of accident
le sauvetage en mer	sea rescue
le gilet de sauvetage	life jacket
les sapeurs-pompiers	fire department
Donnez-moi votre nom et votre adresse.	Give me your name and address.
. . . votre premis de conduire	. . . your driver's license
la police d'assurance	insurance policy
faire un constat	fill out an accident report form
la contravention	fine
Vous étiez en tort.	You were in the wrong.
C'est de votre faute.	It's your fault
Je voudrais signaler un vol.	I'd like to report a theft.
J'ai perdu/On m'a volé . . .	I've lost/Somebody's stolen . . .
. . . ma clé/mon argent/	. . . my key/my money/
mon portefeuille/	my wallet/
mon porte-monnaie/mon sac/	my change purse/my bag/
mon appareil-photo	my camera
Je suis désolé.	I'm sorry.
Tout va s'arranger.	It'll all get sorted out.
Je suis en retard.	I'm late.

the way it works

More about the past tense

Here are some examples of verbs which use **être** to form the past tense:

1 Le docteur **est arrivé** de bonne heure. The doctor arrived early.
2 Julien **est tombé** dans l'eau. Julien fell in the water.
3 Claire **est allée** au bureau de poste pour téléphoner. Claire went to the post office to make a phone call.

You will notice from this last example that with verbs using **être** in the past tense, the past participle has to agree with the subject of the verb. Luckily, only a small number of verbs take **être** and those that do can be easily learned. Here is a list of most of them, together with their past participles:

aller (to go)	allé	**partir** (to depart)	parti
arriver (to arrive)	arrivé	**rester** (to stay)	resté
descendre (to go down)	descendu	**retourner** (to return)	retourné
entrer (to enter)	entré	**sortir** (to go out)	sorti
monter (to go up)	monté	**tomber** (to fall)	tombé
mourir (to die)	mort	**(re)venir** (to come (back))	(re)venu

Reflexive verbs in the past tense

Reflexive verbs use **être** in the past tense:

Julien **s'est levé** de bonne heure.	Julien got up early.
Claire **s'est réveillée** peu après.	Claire woke up soon afterwards.
Ils **se sont habillés**.	They got dressed.

Note also ways of saying "I have hurt myself," etc.

Je **me suis fait** mal.	I have hurt myself.
Je **me suis tordu** la jambe.	I have twisted my leg.
Je **me suis coupé** le doigt.	I have cut my finger.

things to do

3 You are at the gas station. Tell the attendant in French:
  (a) to fill the tank
  (b) that you want 25 liters of super
  (c) to give you some oil
  (d) to give you some water for the battery
  (e) that you want to check the tire pressure

4 You are at a garage. Tell the attendant:
  (a) you have broken down
  (b) your car won't start
  (c) your brakes are not working

Ask him if he runs a road service,
and say you are in a hurry (*Je suis
pressé(e)*) because you're already late.

5 1 You see the street sign **SENS INTERDIT**. What does it mean?
  (a) no parking   **(b)** no entry   **(c)** no passing
2 You've been involved in a collision and need to sort out some details.
  Can you remember the French for:
  (a) name and address   **(b)** driver's license   **(c)** insurance policy
  (d) accident report form
3 What does the sign **SORTIE DE SECOURS** mean?
  (a) first aid   **(b)** strong room   **(c)** emergency exit

SPORTS AND LEISURE

au centre des sports/at the sports complex

Julien and Claire arrive at the sports complex and consult the program of activities.

Claire: Voyons . . . Qu'est-ce qu'on peut faire ici? (reads) Badminton, tennis, natation, judo, danse, tir à l'arc, mini-golf—ah, j'adore ça. **Tu aimes le mini-golf?**

Julien: **Non, pas du tout. Je joue au badminton** et au tennis, mais pas aujourd'hui à cause de ma jambe. **J'aime bien nager** mais le judo—je n'en sais rien . . . (He sees another notice) Aha, regarde, Claire, tu vois **il y a un match de football** au grand stade cet après-midi. **J'ai envie d'y aller.**

Claire: **Ça ne m'intéresse pas** du tout. Toi, **tu vas assister au match** et moi je **vais jouer au golf**, d'accord?

Julien: OK. (Looks at his watch) Le match commence à deux heures. Je vais te quitter maintenant. On se rencontrera ici à quatre heures et demie.

Claire: Bon, d'accord. A tout à l'heure.

64

At the sports center

Qu'est-ce qu'on peut faire ici?	What can one do here?
la natation, la danse, le tir à l'arc	swimming, dancing, archery
Tu aimes le mini-golf?	Do you like miniature golf?
Pas du tout.	Not at all.
Je joue au badminton/au tennis.	I play badminton/tennis.
pas aujourd'hui	not today
à cause de ma jambe	because of my leg
J'aime bien nager.	I like swimming very much.
Je n'en sais rien.	I don't know anything about it.
Il y a un match de football.	There is a soccer game.
J'ai envie d'y aller.	I would like to go.
Ça ne m'intéresse pas.	That doesn't interest me.
Tu vas assister au match.	You go and watch the game.
Je vais jouer au mini-golf.	I'm going to play miniature golf.
Je vais te quitter maintenant.	I'll leave you now.
On se rencontrera ici.	We'll meet here.
A tout à l'heure.	See you later.

Sports and games

Je vais jouer . . . I'm going to play.
J'aime faire du/de la . . . I enjoy...
Je voudrais louer une raquette.
   I'd like to rent a racket.
Je voudrais un abonnement/
   un permis pour une semaine.
   I'd like a season ticket/
   permit for one week.
Je voudrais prendre des leçons.
   I'd like to take some lessons.

l'après-midi

SIGHTSEEING

Museums You normally pay an entrance fee for national museums, with a 50% discount on Sundays. Children, students and senior citizens pay less. Some museums are free on Wednesdays or Sundays. All museums are closed at Easter (**Pâcques**), Christmas (**Noël**), and other public holidays (**Jours Fériés**), and most close on Tuesdays.

There are many national and local festivals. The tourist office (**Syndicat d'Initiative**) will be able to give you details of these and any other local events, exhibitions, concerts, etc.

un après-midi libre/an afternoon off

Bernard and Martine are planning how to spend their afternoon.

Bernard:	**Qu'est-ce que tu voudrais faire** cet après-midi, chérie?
Martine:	**J'aimerais bien aller au Centre Pompidou.** Je n'y suis jamais allée.
Bernard:	Au Centre Pompidou—**c'est une bonne idée.** Ils ont toujours de belles expositions de photographie là-bas.
Martine:	**Moi je préfère les expositions d'art moderne.**
Bernard:	Il y a quelque chose pour tous les goûts au Centre Pompidou. Et ce soir **on pourra peut-être aller à un concert.**
Martine:	**Oui, ça me plairait beaucoup.**
(At the Pompidou Center)	
Martine:	Aha Renseignements . . . (reading aloud) Regarde—samedi le vingt et un mars, c'est aujourd'hui, n'est-ce-pas? Il y a un concert de musique française à vingt heures trente. Les tickets sont à 40 francs.
Bernard:	C'est de la musique classique, crois-tu?
Martine:	Mais oui, bien sûr. De la bonne musique.
Bernard:	**J'aime mieux** trouver un autre concert—du jazz, peut-être. . .
Martine:	**Je déteste** le jazz.
Bernard:	Et moi, **J'ai horreur de** la musique classique.
Martine:	Allons prendre un verre à la cafétéria du cinquième étage, et discutons ça un peu.

ENTERTAINMENT

▶ **Le cinéma** Many American and British films are shown in France, either with subtitles (the more serious) or dubbed (Westerns, thrillers, etc). Look in the newspapers (**la page des spectacles**) or entertainment guides for details. Performances (which are not usually continuous) run from about 2 p.m. (**la première séance**) to a late showing at 10 p.m. It is unusual to be able to buy tickets in advance. The usher (**l'ouvreuse**) will expect a tip after showing you to your seat.

une soirée au cinéma/an evening at the movies

Patrick and Sylvie decide to go to the movies.

Patrick: **Tu aimerais aller au cinéma** ce soir?

Sylvie: **Oui, avec plaisir. Quel film voudrais-tu voir?**

Patrick: Oh, **Je ne sais pas, ça m'est égal. J'aime bien les westerns,** et toi?

Sylvie: Moi, **je préfère les films d'aventure,** ou les films policiers—même les films de science-fiction. Consultons la page des spectacles.

(They look at the entertainment page.)

Patrick: Voilà . . . Cinéma . . . Que penses-tu de ce film de Woody Allen?

Sylvie: Oh non, **ça ne me dit rien.** Mais regarde! On joue un Tati à La Lumière. **J'aimerais bien voir ça.**

Patrick: Bon, allons-y. **A quelle heure commence la première séance** du soir?

Sylvie: **Elle commence à sept heures** et à La Lumière on peut réserver les billets d'avance.

What would you like to do?

Qu'est-ce que tu voudrais faire?	What would you like to do?
J'aimerais bien aller . . .	I'd like to go . . .
Je n'y suis jamais allée.	I've never been there.
C'est une bonne idée.	It's a good idea.
Tu aimerais aller au cinéma?	Would you like to go to the movies?
Quel film voudrais-tu voir?	What film would you like to see?
Ça m'est égal.	I don't care/It's all the same to me.

Ça te dirait d'aller au théâtre?	Would you like to go to the theater?
Si on allait au musée?	Shall we go to the museum?
On pourrait aller à un concert.	We could go to a concert.
J'aimerais bien voir ça.	I'd love to see that.
J'ai grande envie d'y aller.	I'd really like to go.
Oui, avec plaisir.	Yes, I'd love to.
Ça me plairait beaucoup.	

Going to an art gallery (le musée d'art) or exhibition

une belle exposition de photographie	a beautiful photography exhibit
une exposition d'art moderne	a modern art exhibit
quelque chose pour tous les goûts	something for all tastes
la peinture	painting
une œuvre	work of art
le peintre	painter
le dessin	drawing

Going to a concert, ballet or opera

la salle de concert	concert hall
le concert de musique classique/pop	concert of classical music/pop music
le concert de jazz	jazz concert
les chanteurs	singers
l'orchestre	orchestra
les solistes	soloists

Going to the movies or theater

un film d'aventure/de science-fiction	an adventure/science fiction film
un film policier/un western	a detective film/a western
un dessin animé	a cartoon
un film doublé/avec sous-titres	a dubbed film/film with subtitles
V.O.—version originale	undubbed foreign film
V.F.—version française	foreign film which has been dubbed
passer un film/jouer un film	to show a film
A quelle heure commence . . .	What time does . . . begin?
le film principal	the feature film
la première séance	the first session
le spectacle?	the performance
Faut-il donner un pourboire à l'ouvreuse?	Should one tip the usher?

Asking someone's opinion

Que pensez-vous du nouveau film de Spielberg?	What do you think of Spielberg's new film?
Comment trouves-tu le théâtre français?	How do you like the French theater?
Tu aimes la musique classique?	Do you like classical music?
Ça te plaît, les expositions de photographie?	Do you like photography exhibits?

Giving your opinion of something

J'aime les westerns.	I like westerns.
J'aime bien les musées.	I like museums very much.
J'adore le ballet russe.	I love the Russian ballet.
Ça me plaît, les matchs de football.	I like soccer games.
Ça m'ennuie, le mini-golf.	I find miniature golf boring.
Je préfère le tennis.	I prefer tennis.
J'aime mieux les films policiers.	I prefer detective films.
Ça ne me dit rien.	That doesn't interest me.
Je n'aime pas la musique pop.	I don't like pop music.
Je n'aime pas du tout le rugby.	I don't like rugby at all.
Je déteste le jazz.	I hate jazz.
J'ai horreur de l'opéra.	I hate opera.
Discutons ça un peu.	Let's talk about it.

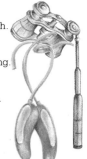

Buying tickets for concerts, theaters, museums, etc.

Y a-t-il des places?	Are there any seats?
Peut-on acheter des billets d'avance?	Can you buy tickets in advance?
Je voudrais réserver des places.	I would like to reserve some seats.
Il reste quelques places.	There are a few seats left.
Combien coûtent les places au balcon?	How much are the seats in the balcony?
. . . au parterre/à l'orchestre?	. . . on the ground floor?
. . . à la seconde galerie?	. . . in the second balcony?
Je voudrais deux tickets de 40 francs.	I'd like two tickets for 40 francs.
Des retours de dernière minute.	Last-minute returns.
Combien coûtent les billets?	How much are the tickets?
Y a-t-il des réductions pour . . . ?	Are there any discounts for . . .?
. . . les enfants/les étudiants?	. . . children/students?
. . . les retraités/les chômeurs?	. . . retired people/unemployed people?
Avez-vous un guide?	Do you have a guidebook?
entrée libre	entrance free

Opening times (Heures d'ouverture)

Ouvert . . . /Fermé . . .	Open . . . /Closed . . .
A quelle heure est-ce que ça ouvre?	What time does it open?
A quelle heure est-ce que ça ferme?	What time does it close?
Est-ce que le musée est ouvert le mardi?	Is the museum open on Tuesdays?

Dates

Quelle est la date aujourd'hui?	What is the date today?
C'est . . .	It's . . .
samedi le vingt et un mars	Saturday, March 21st
le premier avril	April 1st
le deux juin	June 2nd
le onze novembre	November 11th (Veteran's Day)
le quatorze juillet	July 14th (Bastille Day)
le vingt-cinq décembre	December 25th
mille neuf cent quatre-vingt-douze	1992

the way it works

In the future

When you are talking about something that is going to happen later on, then you are using the future tense. In French you can do this in two ways. You can use the verb **aller** with another verb in the infinitive, just as in English:

Cet après-midi, **je vais jouer** au golf. This afternoon I am going to play golf.

Alternatively, you can add the following endings to the infinitive of the verb to indicate the future:

-ai	je jouer**ai** (I will play)	**-ons**	nous visiter**ons** (we will visit)
-as	tu donner**as** (you will give)	**-ez**	vous finir**ez** (you will finish)
-a	il écouter**a** (he will listen)	**-ont**	elles rencontrer**ont** (they will meet)

Some verbs which end in **-e** drop the **-e** before adding the future endings:

attendre: j'attendr**ai**   prendre: elle prendr**a**
dire: nous dir**ons**

There are quite a number of verbs which are irregular in the future and these have to be learned. Here are some common ones:

aller:	j'**irai**	faire:	je **ferai**
avoir:	j'**aurai**	pouvoir:	je **pourrai**
être:	je **serai**	vouloir:	je **voudrai**

Negative expressions

In order to say *only, no one, never, nothing* and *no more* in French you have to use the negative expressions **ne . . . que, ne . . . personne, ne . . . jamais, ne . . . rien**, and **ne . . . plus**.

Je **n'**ai **que** 40 francs.	I have only 40 francs.
Elle **ne** voit **personne**.	She sees no one (doesn't see anyone).
Tu **ne** vas **jamais** au cinéma.	You never go to the movies.
Vous **ne** dites **rien**.	You say nothing (don't say anything).
Je **n'**ai **plus** d'argent.	I have no more money.
Il **n'**est **plus** là.	He is no longer there.

things to do

6.1 Say what you do and and don't like doing in your spare time. Use one of the following expressions: **J'aime bien/J'aime/Je n'aime pas/Je déteste.**

A la maison
1 regarder la télé
2 écouter la radio (listen to radio)
3 jouer aux cartes
4 faire du jardinage (garden)
5 faire la cuisine (cook)

Sports et loisirs
1 faire du vélo
2 jouer au tennis
3 aller à la pêche
4 faire de la voile
5 faire du ski

6.2 And say what you think of each of the following. Use **ça me plaît, j'aime mieux/ça ne m'intéresse pas/ça m'ennuie/j'ai horreur de**
1 le ballet—le théâtre—le cinéma—la musique classique
2 le football—la natation—le cyclisme—la varappe

6.3 Can you match the following questions and answers?

1 Elle habite seule? (*lives alone*)
2 Tu n'aimes pas les moules?
3 Encore 3 francs, s'il vous plaît.
4 Elles ne mangent pas de viande?
5 Tu n'as pas soif aujourd'hui?

(a) Non, elles ne mangent que des légumes et des fruits.
(b) Non, merci, je ne bois rien.
(c) Oui et elle ne voit personne.
(d) Non, je ne les mange jamais.
(e) Je m'excuse, je n'ai plus d'argent.

6.4 Qu'est-ce que tu voudrais faire ce soir?

e.g., Tu aimerais aller au théâtre?   Oui, j'aimerais bien aller au théâtre.
Non, je ne peux pas sortir ce soir.

How would you deal with the following invitations?

1 Tu aimerais aller au match?
2 Tu as envie d'aller au cinéma?
3 Si on allait au centre des sports?
4 Ça te dirait d'aller à l'opéra?
5 Tu voudrais aller au musée?

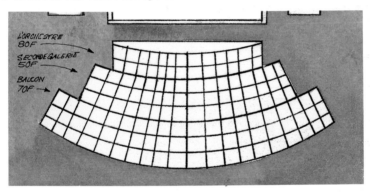

6.5
1 Ask if there are any tickets for tonight's performance.
2 Ask if you can buy tickets for tonight's performance.
3 Ask if you can reserve two tickets in the balcony.
4 Ask if they give a discount for students.
5 Ask for three tickets on the ground floor with a discount for tomorrow.
6 Ask how much it comes to.

6.6
1 What is being advertised here?
2 What date does it close?
3 Where is it?
4 What time does it open and close?
5 Is it closed on Sundays?
6 What price are the tickets?

Vocabulary

la faïence   earthenware

> **Expositions**
>
> **400 ANS D'ART :
> FAIENCES
> ET PORCELAINES
> DES PROVINCES
> FRANÇAISES**
>
> à l'abbaye de DAOULAS,
> dans le Finistère (29224).
>
> Jusqu'au 31 août 1987,
> de 10 heures à 19 heures,
> tous les jours sans exception.
>
> Abbaye de Daoulas,
> place de l'Église, 29224 Daoulas.
> Entrée 25 F. Tél. 98.25.84.39.

71

CONVERSATION

Talking about yourself/The weather

une réception

Patrick, Bernard, Martine and Sylvie have been invited to a reception on the last day of the trade fair.

Bernard:	(to Patrick) **Je vous présente M. Alain Lemonnier, un collégue Lyonnais.** Patrick Vincent—Alain Lemonnier.
Patrick:	Enchanté de faire votre connaissance.
Bernard:	**Vous connaissez ma femme,** Martine?
Alain:	Non, pas encore. Enchanté, madame.
Patrick:	Vous êtes dessinateur aussi, Alain?
Alain:	Non, **je suis architecte.**
Patrick:	Ah, c'est intéressant. Ma fiancée fait ses études en architecture. Elle est étudiante à l'Université de Londres.
Bernard:	Ah, voilà Sylvie. Alain, **permettez-moi de vous présenter** Mlle Sylvie Corentin, une de nos meilleures programmeuses. **Elle travaille dans notre bureau à Rouen.**
Alain:	(to Martine) Et vous, madame **qu'est-ce que vous faites comme travail**? Vous êtes dans les affaires aussi?
Martine:	Non, je suis professeur dans une école maternelle. J'ai deux enfants, donc **Je travaille à mi-temps.**
Président:	(clearing his throat loudly) Mesdames et Messieurs, c'est un grand plaisir pour moi de vous accueillir ici ce soir. J'espère que tout le monde passera une soirée agréable . . .

un barbecue sur la plage/a beach barbecue

It is Sunday evening and the beach barbecue is in full swing.

Agathe: Quelle belle soirée. **Il fait toujours si beau temps** à S. Jean.

Henri: Oui, mais la météo prévoit des orages pour demain. La pluie va commencer pendant la nuit . . .

Agathe: Regarde les enfants. Ils s'amusent bien, n'est-ce pas?

(On another part of the beach . . .)

Thierry: Salut, Claire. Tiens, tu es anglaise! Tu habites à Londres?

Claire: Non, j'habite à Liverpool. Et toi?

Thierry: **Je vais au collège** à Tours. J'étudie pour devenir ingénieur.

Claire: Et **tu sais jouer de la guitare?**

Thierry: Oui, je joue dans un groupe à Tours. Dis, Claire, **Tu restes longtemps en France?**

Claire: Deux mois, environ.

Thierry: Et ça te plaît ici?

Claire: Oui, **ça me plaît beaucoup**. J'aime bien le soleil, et **il fait soleil tous les jours** à S. Jean-sur-Mer.

Introductions

Je vous présente M. Alain Lemonnier.	I'd like to introduce you to M. Alain Lemonnier.
un collègue Lyonnais	a colleague from Lyon
Permettez-moi de vous présenter . . .	Allow me to introduce . . .
Laissez-moi vous présenter . . .	Let me introduce . . .
une de nos meilleures programmeuses	one of our best computer programmers
Elle travaille dans notre bureau à Rouen.	She works in our Rouen office.
Vous connaissez ma femme, Martine?	Do you know my wife, Martine?
Enchanté(e) de faire votre connaissance.	Delighted to meet you.
Enchanté(e), Madame.	Delighted.
Salut, Claire!	Hello, Claire!
C'est un grand plaisir pour moi de vous accueillir ici ce soir . . .	It is a pleasure for me to welcome you here tonight . . .

Talking about jobs

Que faites-vous (dans la vie)?	What do you do?
Qu'est-ce que vous faites comme travail?	What work do you do?
Vous êtes dessinateur aussi?*	Are you a designer too?
Vous êtes dans les affaires aussi?	Are you in business too?
Non, je suis architecte.	No, I'm an architect.
Je suis professeur dans une école maternelle.	I'm a teacher in a nursery school.
Ma fiancée fait ses études en architecture.	My fiancée is studying architecture.
Elle est étudiante à l'Université de Londres.	She's a student at London University.
J'étudie pour devenir ingénieur.	I'm studying to become an engineer.
Je suis étudiant(e).	I'm a student.
Je vais au collège.	I go to high school.
Je suis femme au foyer.	I'm a homemaker.
Je travaille chez moi/à la maison.	I work at home.
Je travaille à mi-temps.	I work part-time.
Je suis chômeur/se.	I'm unemployed.

*Note in French, you leave out the equivalent of a/an when talking about your job.

The weather

le bulletin météorologique	weather forecast
la température	the temperature
une averse	shower
à l'ombre	in the shade
Quelle belle soirée.	What a lovely evening.
Il fait toujours si beau temps . . .	It's always so nice . . .
La météo prévoit des orages.	According to the forecast there are going to be storms.
La pluie va commencer pendant la nuit.	The rain will start during the night.
Il fait du soleil tous les jours.	It's sunny every day.
Quel temps fait-il?	What's the weather like?
Il fait beau temps/mauvais temps.	The weather is good/bad.
Il fait chaud/froid.	It's warm/cold.
Il fait du soleil.	It's sunny.
Le temps est ensoleillé.	It's sunny.
Le ciel se découvre.	It's clearing up.
Il est couvert/nuageux.	It's overcast/cloudy.
Il pleut/grêle.	It's raining/hailing.
Il fait du vent.	It's windy.
Il y a des orages.	It's stormy.
Il fait du brouillard/de la brume.	It's foggy/misty.
Il gèle/neige.	It's freezing/snowing.

18

Savez-vous jouer un instrument? (Can you play an instrument?)

Tu sais jouer de la guitare?	Can you play the guitar?
Je joue du piano/du violon.	I play the piano/violin.

Talking about your stay

Je suis ici en vacances/en voyage d'affaires/pour perfectionner la langue.	I'm here on vacation/on a business trip/to improve my French (the language).
Tu restes longtemps en France?	Are you staying long in France?
Combien de temps restez-vous en France?	How long are you staying in France?
Depuis combien de temps êtes-vous ici?	How long have you been here?
Deux mois, environ.	About two months.
six semaines/quinze jours	six weeks/two weeks
Je reste en France pendant huit jours	I'm staying in France for a week
Je suis ici depuis la fin de juillet/le mois dernier/la semaine dernière.	I've been here since the end of July/last month/last week.
C'est votre première visite ici?	Is it your first visit here?
Où logez-vous?	Where are you staying?
Ça te plaît ici?	Do you like it here?
Vous vous plaisez ici?	Do you like it here?
Oui, ça me plaît beaucoup.	Yes, very much.
Quand partez-vous?	When are you leaving?
Je pars demain/lundi/la semaine prochaine/le mois prochain/au début d'octobre.	I'm leaving tomorrow/on Monday/next week/next month/at the beginning of October.

USEFUL WORDS AND PHRASES

pas encore	not yet
c'est intéressant	it's interesting
J'espère que tout le monde passera une soirée agréable.	I hope that everyone will have a pleasant evening.
Voilà Thierry qui arrive.	Here comes Thierry.
ce garçon-là	that boy
Tiens!	Well!/So!

the way it works

Savoir and connaître

savoir *to know*		connaître *to know*	
je **sais**	nous **savons**	je **connais**	nous **connaissons**
tu **sais**	vous **savez**	tu **connais**	vous **connaissez**
il/elle **sait**	ils/elles **savent**	il/elle **connaît**	ils/elles **connaissent**

Savoir and **connaître** both mean *to know* in French. Use **connaître** for knowing a person, a place, etc.:

Vous connaissez ma femme, Martine?	Do you know my wife, Martine?
Je ne connais pas cette ville.	I don't know this town.

Savoir is used for knowing how to do something, or knowing a fact (e.g., I know that . . .):

Tu sais jouer de la guitare?	Do know how to play the guitar?
Je sais que tu as raison.	I know you're right.

How to say bigger, better, etc.

To say something is bigger, smaller and so on, use **plus** together with the adjective, e.g.:

une **grande** réception	a large reception
une **plus grande** réception	a larger reception
la **plus grande** réception	the largest reception

The adjective "good" however is a bit different:

une **bonne** programmeuse	a good programmer
une **meilleure** programmeuse	a better programmer
la **meilleure** programmeuse	the best programmer

Note also how the adverb **bien** changes to **mieux**:

Julien joue très **bien** de la guitare.	Julien plays the guitar very well.
Oui, mais Thierry joue **mieux**.	Yes, but Thierry plays better.
Mais moi, je joue **le mieux!**	But I play best!

things to do

7.1 Everyone is talking about where they work and what they do. Answer the questions affirmatively, e.g., Vous travaillez dans une école? Oui, je suis professeur. (See p. 83 for vocabulary.)

1 Vous travaillez dans un bureau?
2 Vous allez au collège?
3 Vous travaillez dans un hôpital?
4 Vous travaillez dans un garage?
5 Vous travaillez dans un magasin?
6 Vous travaillez dans une pharmacie?

7.2 You are being asked about your visit to Belgium. Can you answer these questions in French?

1 D'où venez-vous, monsieur/madame? [Say that you come from London.]
2 Vous restez longtemps en Belgique? [You're staying about ten days.]
3 C'est votre première visite ici? [No, it's your second visit.]
4 Ça vous plaît à Bruxelles? [Yes, you like it very much.]
5 Alors, je vous invite à dîner demain soir. [Thank him/her very much.]

7.3 Quel temps fait-il aujourd'hui? Look at the weather map.

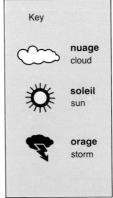
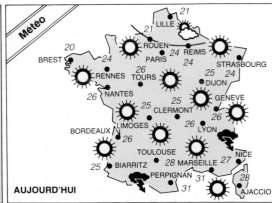

1 Quel temps fait-il à Rouen?
2 Quel temps fait-il à Lille?
3 Quel temps fait-il aux Alpes et aux Pyrénées?
4 Quelle est la température à Marseille?
5 Quelle est la température à Genève?

7.4   *Le temps aujourd'hui*

«Il fera beau temps en général en France pendant le matin; toutefois, des nuages s'étendront* progressivement aux régions du nord. Dans le sud, le temps restera chaud et il y aura beaucoup de soleil.

L'après-midi sera agréable et légèrement moins** chaud sur la Bretagne, le Nord, la Normandie et le Bassin parisien.

Sur l'Aquitaine, le Massif Central et Midi-Pyrénées il y aura des orages très isolés dans la soirée et la nuit.

Les températures atteindront 23°C à 28°F au nord de la Loire et 28°C à 30°C au sud; 32°C près des Pyrénées et en Provence.»

* will spread   ** slightly less

1 According to the forecast, what will the weather be like in general during the morning?
2 What is likely to happen in the north, however?
3 In what way is this different from in the south?
4 What weather is forecast for Brittany in the afternoon?
5 Where and when are there likely to be scattered storms?
6 What temperatures are expected south of the Loire?

NORD

OUEST◄──┼──► EST

SUD

7.5 See if you can fill in this form giving details about yourself in French.

Nom (last name)..
Prénom (first name) ....
Date de naissance (date of birth) ....
Lieu de naissance (place of birth) ....
Signe astrologique (sign of the zodiac) ....
Situation de famille (marital status) ....
[marié(e)/divorcé(e)/séparé(e)/célibataire; frère(s)/sœur(s)/ enfant(s)]*
Profession ....
Lieu de travail ....
Hobbies ....
Sports préférés ....
Aime ....
Déteste ....
Rêve (dream) ....
Angoisse (worry/anxiety) ....
* *Rayer la mention inutile* (delete where applicable)

1.1 1 Bonjour, monsieur; au revoir, monsieur. 2 Bonjour, madame; au revoir, madame. 3 Bonjour, madame; au revoir, madame. 4 Bonjour, mademoiselle; au revoir, mademoiselle. 5 Salut, Damien!; au revoir, Damien.

1.2 1 Oui, je suis Madame Valéry. 2 Je m'appelle Monsieur/Madame . . . 3 Enchanté(e) de faire votre connaissance, madame. 4 Très bien merci, madame. 5 Ça va bien, merci.

1.3 1 Oui, c'est ma valise. 2 Oui, c'est mon taxi. 3 Oui, c'est ma voiture. 4 Oui, c'est mon fils. 5 Oui, c'est mon nom. 6 Oui, ce sont mes bagages. 7 Oui, c'est mon passeport.

1.4 1 salle de bains. 2 une chambre avec salle de bains et WC. 3 une chambre avec douche. 4 une chambre à deux lits. 5 une chambre à un grand lit. 6 une chambre à un lit. Elle voudrait une chambre à un grand lit, avec douche et cabinet de toilette.

1.5 2 Oui, la valise est dans le coffre. 3 Oui, la clé est dans la porte. 4 Oui, la tente est sous les arbres. 5 Oui, la douche est dans la salle de bains. 6 Oui, le passeport est dans le sac.

1.6 2 Non, elle n'est pas dans le coffre. 3 Non, elle n'est pas dans la porte. 4 Non, elle n'est pas sous les arbres. 5 Non, elle n'est pas dans la salle de bains. 6 Non, il n'est pas dans le sac.

1.7 2 Non, elle est petite. 3 Non, il est petit. 4 Non, il est petit. 5 Non, il est petit.

1.8 2 François, vous avez la chambre cinq au troisième étage. 3 Nathalie, vous avez la chambre dix au deuxième étage. 4 Christian, vous avez la chambre deux au rez-de-chaussée. 5 Florence, vous avez la chambre quatorze au quatrième étage.

2.1 1 Je voudrais du café et des croissants. 2 Je voudrais du pain, du beurre, de la confiture et du thé. 3 Je voudrais une tasse de thé. 4 Je voudrais un jus d'orange et un yaourt. 5 Je voudrais du thé avec du pain et du beurre.

2.2 1 trois heures moins cinq *or* deux heures cinquante-cinq. 2 trois heures cinq. 3 trois heures et quart. 4 trois

heures moins le quart *or* deux heures quarante-cinq. 5 une heure. 6 trois heures vingt.

2.3 You: A quelle heure est le prochain train pour Paris?
You: Combien de temps faut-il pour aller de Boulogne à Paris?
You: Le train arrive à quelle heure?
You: Faut-il changer?

2.4 2 Il voudrait un (billet) aller simple à Lyon, en première class. 3 Ils voudraient deux (billets) aller-retour à Avignon, en deuxième classe. 4 Il voudrait un (billet) aller-retour à Bordeaux, en deuxième classe. 5 Ils voudraient deux (billets) aller simple à Nice, en première classe.

2.5 e.g. (a) Pour aller à la gare, s.v.p? (b) Où est le parc? (c) Est-ce qu'il y a un restaurant près d'ici? (d) Où est la rue du Port, s.v.p? (e) Où est la poste, s.v.p? (f) S'il vous plaît, monsieur, la station de métro? (g) Pour aller à la plage, s.v.p? (h) Pour aller à l'hôtel, s.v.p? (i) S'il vous plaît, madame, où est l'arrêt d'autobus? (j) Est-ce qu'il y a une boulangerie près d'ici?

2.6 1 le stade. 2 la banque. 3 le cinéma. 4 la bibliothèque. 5 le syndicat d'initiative. 6 le théâtre.

3.1 1 (b). 2 (c). 3 (a). 4 (e). 5 (d). 6 (h). 7 (f). 8 (g).

3.2 Je n'aime pas la couleur. Pouvez-vous me montrer une autre couleur—gris ou brun, peut-être? . . . Ce blouson est trop grand. Avez-vous quelque chose de plus petit? . . . Oui, s'il vous plaît. Il me va bien. C'est combien? . . . Je le prends.

3.3 Non, elle est trop petite. . . . Non, elle est trop grande. . . . Non, il est trop court. . . . Non, il est trop long. . . . Non, elles sont trop petites.

3.4 1 (e). 2 (d). 3 (b). 4 (a). 5 (c).

3.5 250 grams of butter, a piece of cheese, ½ kilo of granulated sugar, a liter of milk, 200 grams of paté, 4 slices of ham, a can of fish soup, a kilo of apples, a pound of pears, ½ liter of vinegar, 100 grams of Russian salad, a carton of grated carrots, a container of ground coffee, 2 bottles of red wine, a dozen eggs.

3.6 Deux baguettes, s.v.p. . . . Je voudrais aussi quatre croissants, deux brioches et une tarte aux pommes. . . . C'est combien?

3.7 *(starting from top left going clockwise)* Pour monsieur, les huîtres, et après, un bifteck avec des pommes frites, et un verre de vin rouge. Pour madame, l'assiette de fruits de mer et du poulet, avec du vin blanc—pas de pommes de terre. Pour monsieur, des cuisses de grenouille, du porc, et une bière. Et apportez-lui une salade verte avec le porc, s.v.p. Pour mademoiselle, une tarte aux pommes, une glace et un cola. Pour monsieur des frites et un jus d'orange. Pour madame le consommé, et après la truite. Et à boire, une bouteille d'eau minérale, s.v.p.

3.8 Example: Je prends un croque-monsieur, s.v.p. . . . Un café crème. Je prends un hamburger, s.v.p. . . . Une pression.

4.1 1 (b), 2 (c), 3 (e), 4 (a), 5 (f), 6 (d).

4.2 Celui-ci, s'il vous plaît. Celle-là, s'il vous plaît. Celui-ci, s'il vous plaît. Celui-ci et celui-là, s'il vous plaît.

4.3 Je voudrais des timbres, s'il vous plaît. Je voudrais envoyer une lettre et deux cartes postales. La lettre est pour l'Angleterre, et les cartes postales sont pour les Etats-Unis. Non, je voudrais (aussi) envoyer un colis à Paris.

4.4 1 Quel est le taux de change aujourd'hui? 2 Est-ce que je peux encaisser un chèque? 3 Je voudrais encaisser cinquante dollars de chèques de voyage. 4 Je voudrais changer un billet de cent francs pour dix pièces de dix francs.

4.5 C'est bien le 87-23-25? Je voudrais parler à M. Lotte, s'il vous plaît. C'est . . . Est-ce qu'il peut me téléphoner?/Pouvez-vous lui dire de me téléphoner? C'est le numéro . . . Au revoir, madame.

4.6 2 Bernard lui dit "Bonjour." 3 Le caissier lui donne un billet de 100F. 4 Elle lui téléphone. 5 Elle leur écrit.

5.1 1 Il a mal au dos. 2 Il a mal à la tête. 3 Il a mal aux oreilles. 4 Il a mal au doigt. 5 Il a mal au ventre. 6 Il a mal à la jambe.

5.2 1 (b), 2 (c), 3 (c), 4 (a).

5.3 (a) Faites le plein, s'il vous plaît. (b) Je voudrais/Donnez-moi vingt-cinq litres d'essence super, s'il vous plaît. (c) Donnez-moi de l'huile. (d) Donnez-moi de l'eau pour la batterie. (e) Je voudrais vérifier la pression des pneus.

5.4 (a) Je suis en panne. (b) Ma voiture ne démarre pas. (c) Mes freins ne marchent pas. Est-ce que vous avez un service de dépannage? Je suis pressé(e)—je suis déjà en retard.

5.5 1 (b). 2 (a) Votre/Mon nom et votre/mon adresse, (b) votre permis de conduire, (c) votre police d'assurance, (d) un constat. 3 (c).

6.1 *A la maison:* e.g., J'aime écouter la radio, j'aime faire du jardinage, je n'aime pas faire la cuisine, je déteste regarder la télé. *Sports et loisirs:* e.g., J'aime bien faire du vélo, j'aime aller à la pêche, je n'aime pas faire du ski, je déteste faire de la voile.

6.2 e.g., 1 Ça me plaît, le ballet. Ça m'ennuie, la musique classique. Ça ne m'intéresse pas, le cinéma. J'ai horreur du théâtre.

6.3 1 (c). 2 (d). 3 (e). 4 (a). 5 (b).

6.4 e.g., 1 Non, ça ne m'intéresse pas le football. 2 Oui, je voudrais bien y aller. 3 Non, je ne peux pas sortir ce matin. 4 Oh non, j'ai horreur de l'opéra. 5 Oui, avec plaisir.

6.5 1 Y a-t-il des places pour ce soir? 2 Peut-on acheter des billets pour le spectacle? 3 Je voudrais réserver deux places au balcon. 4 Y a-t-il des réductions pour les étudiants? 5 Je voudrais trois billets à l'orchestre avec réduction pour demain. 6 Ça fait combien, s.v.p?

6.6 1 An exhibition of French china. 2 August 31. 3 Daoulas Abbey, Finistère. 4 Opens 10 a.m., closes 7 p.m. 5 No. 6 25 F.

7.1 1 Oui, je suis secrétaire/journaliste/programmeur/se, etc. 2 Oui, je suis étudiant(e). 3 Oui, je suis médecin/infirmière. 4 Oui, je suis

mécanicien. 5 Oui, je suis vendeur/se. 6 Oui, je suis pharmacien(ne).
7.2 1 Je viens de Londres. 2 Dix jours environ. 3 Non, c'est ma deuxième visite. 4 Oui, ça me plaît beaucoup. 5 Merci beaucoup, monsieur/madame.
7.3 1 Il fait du soleil. 2 Il est nuageux.

3 Il y a des orages. 4 31°, 5 26°.
7.4 1 Fine. 2 Clouds will spread to the north. 3 It will stay warm and sunny in the south. 4 Pleasant and slightly less warm. 5 Aquitaine, the Massif Central and the Midi-Pyrenees. 6 28° to 30°.

English–French topic vocabularies

Numbers 1–99

1	un, une	19	dix-neuf	80	quatre-vingts
2	deux	20	vingt		(4 × 20)
3	trois	21	vingt et un	81	quatre-vingt-un
4	quatre	22	vingt-deux	90	quatre-vingt-dix
5	cinq	23	vingt-trois	99	quatre-vingt-dix-
6	six	24	vingt-quatre		neuf
7	sept	25	vingt-cinq		
8	huit	26	vingt-six		
9	neuf	27	vingt-sept	first	premier/
10	dix	28	vingt-huit		ère
11	onze	29	vingt-neuf	second	deuxième
12	douze	30	trente	third	troisième
13	treize	31	trente et un	fourth	quatrième
14	quatorze	32	trente-deux	fifth	cinquième
15	quinze		etc.	sixth	sixième
16	seize	40	quarante	seventh	septième
17	dix-sept	50	cinquante	eighth	huitième
18	dix-huit	60	soixante	ninth	neuvième
		70	soixante-dix	tenth	dixième

Numbers 100–1000

100	cent
101	cent un
150	cent cinquante
200	deux cents
210	deux cent dix
250	deux cent cinquante
300	trois cents
400	quatre cents
500	cinq cents
600	six cents
700	sept cents
800	huit cents
900	neuf cents
1000	mille

Months/les mois

January	janvier	July	juillet
February	février	August	août
March	mars	September	septembre
April	avril	October	octobre
May	mai	November	novembre
June	juin	December	décembre

Seasons/les saisons

Spring	le printemps
Summer	l'été
Autumn	l'automne
Winter	l'hiver

Clothes

belt	la ceinture	pajamas	le pyjama
blouse	le chemisier	pants	le pantalon
bra	le soutien-gorge	raincoat	l'imperméable (m)
coat	le manteau	scarf	l'écharpe (f)
dress	la robe	shirt	la chemise
gloves	les gants	skirt	la jupe
handbag	le sac à main	socks	les chaussettes (f)
hat	le chapeau	stockings	les bas
jacket	la veste, le blouson	suit (men's)	le complet
jeans	le jean	suit (women's)	le tailleur
nightgown	la chemise de nuit	sweatsuit	le survêtement
overalls	la blouse	swimsuit	le maillot de bain

| T-shirt | le tee-shirt | underpants | le slip |
| tights | le collant | vest | le gilet |

Colors

black	noir
blue	bleu
brown	marron, brun
green	vert
grey	gris
pink	rose
red	rouge
white	blanc(he)
yellow	jaune
dark	foncé
light	clair

Materials

cotton	le coton
leather	le cuir
nylon	le nylon
silk	la soie
straw	la paille
wool	la laine
velvet	le velours

At the pharmacy/à la pharmacie

adhesive bandage	le sparadrap
bandage	le tricostéril
capsule	la gélule
medicine	le médicament
ointment	la pommade
pill, tablet	le comprimé
pharmacy on duty	la pharmacie de service
prescription	l'ordonnance
sleeping pill	le somnifère
suppository	le suppositoire

comb	le peigne
condoms	les préservatifs
disposable diapers	les couches d'enfant
perfume	le parfum
razor blades	les lames de rasoir
sanitary napkins	les serviettes hygiéniques
shampoo	le shampooing
shaving cream	la crème à raser
soap (unscented)	le savon (non parfumé)
suntan oil	l'huile solaire
suntan cream	la crème solaire
tampons	les tampons hygiéniques
toothbrush	la brosse à dents
toothpaste	le dentifrice

Toiletries

| baby food | l'alimentation pour enfants |
| brush | la brosse |

Shopping for food

Fish/les poissons

cod	la morue/le cabillaud
clams	les palourdes
crab	le crabe
crayfish	les écrevisses
hake	le colin
herring	le hareng
lobster	le homard
monkfish	la lotte
mussels	les moules
oysters	les huîtres
prawns	les langoustines
salmon	le saumon
shrimps	les crevettes
skate	la raie

snails	les escargots
sole fillets	les filets de sole
trout	la truite

Meat/les viandes

beef	le bœuf
ham	le jambon
ground meat	la viande hachée
kidneys	les rognons
lamb	l'agneau
pork	le porc
sausages	les saucisses
steak	le bifteck/le steak
veal	le veau

VOCABULARY

Poultry/la volaille

chicken	le poulet
duck	le canard
duckling	le caneton
pheasant	le faisan

Vegetables/les légumes

asparagus	l'asperge
cabbage	le chou
cauliflower	le chou-fleur
carrot	la carotte
celery	le céleri
cucumber	le concombre
endive	l'endive
french fries	les frites
garlic	l'ail
green beans	les haricots verts
kidney beans	les flageolets
leek	le poireau
lettuce	la laitue
mushroom	le champignon
onion	l'oignon
peas	les petits pois
pepper	le poivron (vert)
potato	la pomme de terre
spinach	les épinards
tomato	la tomate

At the bakery/à la boulangerie

bread, loaf	le pain
French bread	la baguette
long, thin loaf	la ficelle
large loaf	le gros pain
whole wheat bread	le pain complet
crescent roll	le croissant
brioche	la brioche
apricot pie	la tarte aux abricots
apple pie	la tarte aux pommes
raisin bread	le pain au raisin

Fruit/les fruits

apple	la pomme
apricot	l'abricot
banana	la banane
blackcurrant	le cassis
cherry	la cerise
grape(s)	le raisin
grapefruit	le pamplemousse
lemon	le citron
orange	l'orange
peach	la pêche
pear	la poire
pineapple	l'ananas
plum	la prune
raspberry	la framboise
strawberry	la fraise

Other groceries

butter	le beurre
cheese	le fromage
coffee	le café
cookies	les biscuits
flour	la farine
margarine	la margarine
milk	le lait
oil	l'huile
pasta	les pâtes
rice	le riz
sugar	le sucre
tea	le thé

Cooking terms

baked	au four
boiled	bouilli
fried	frit
grilled	grillé
smoked	fumé
steamed	à la vapeur
roast	rôti

Sports and games

to do	faire du/de la/de l'
aerobics	l'aérobic
archery	le tir à l'arc
climbing	l'alpinisme/la varappe
cycling	le vélo
dancing	la danse
fishing	la pêche
riding	l'équitation
sailing	la voile
shooting	la chasse
skating	le patinage
skiing	le ski
swimming	la natation
walking	la randonnée
waterskiing	le ski nautique

Equipment

fishing rod	la canne à pêche
racket	la racquette
sailboat	le bateau à voile
skates	les patins
skis	les skis
ski boots	les chaussures de ski
windsurfer	la planche à voile

VOCABULARY

Parts of the body

ankle	la cheville	throat	la gorge
arm	le bras	toe	le doigt de pied
back	le dos	tooth	la dent
chest	la poitrine	wrist	le poignet
ear	l'oreille		
elbow	le coude		

Parts of the car

eye	l'œil	battery	la batterie
eyes	les yeux	brakes	les freins
face	la figure/le visage	bulbs	les ampoules
finger	le doigt	clutch	l'embrayage
foot	le pied	distributor	le distributeur
hair	les cheveux	engine	le moteur
hand	la main	exhaust	le tuyau d'échappement
head	la tête	fan belt	la courroie du ventilateur
heart	le cœur	gas tank	le réservoir d'essence
hip	la hanche	gears	les vitesses
knee	le genou	headlights	les phares
leg	la jambe	ignition	l'allumage
lip	la lèvre	radiator	le radiateur
mouth	la bouche	spark plugs	les bougies
neck	le cou	steering wheel	le volant
nose	le nez	tires	les pneus
skin	la peau	turn signal	l'indicateur
small of back	les reins	wheels	les roues
stomach	le ventre	windshield	le pare-brise
thigh	la cuisse	windshield wipers	les essuie-glace

Professions

accountant	comptable
artist	artiste
banker	banquier
bank teller	employé/e de banque
builder	maçon
businessman	homme d'affaires
businesswoman	femme d'affaires
chef	cuisiner/ière
civil servant	fonctionnaire
company director	directeur/trice
computer programmer	programmeur/cuse
computer operator	opérateur/trice
dentist	dentiste
doctor	médecin
hairdresser	coiffeur/euse
IBM executive	cadre de IBM
interpreter	interprète
journalist	journaliste
lawyer	avocat
mechanic	mécanicien
nurse	infirmière
pharmacist	pharmacien/ne
policeman	agent de police
real estate agent	agent immobilière
sales rep	représentant
secretary	secrétaire
social worker	assistant/e social/e

Workplaces

I work in . . .	Je travaille dans . . .
a bank	une banque
a clinic	une clinique
a factory	une fabrique (small); une usine (large)
a firm	une maison de commerce/une firme
a garage	un garage
a high school	un collège
a hospital	un hôpital
a laboratory	un laboratoire
an office	un bureau
a store	un magasin
a studio	un studio
a workshop	un atelier

VOCABULARY

French-English Vocabulary

à   at; —point   medium (steak)
abbaye *f.*   abbey
accord: d'—   OK, all right
accrochage *m.*   collision
accueillir   welcome
acheter   buy
addition *f.*   check (restaurant)
adorer   love
adresse *f.*   address
aéroport *m.*   airport
affaires *f. pl.*   business
affreux/se   awful
âge *m.*   age
agent *(m.)* de police   police officer
agneau *m.*   lamb
agréable   pleasant
aider   help
ail *m.*   garlic
aimer   like; —mieux   prefer
alcool *m.*   alcohol
alimentation *f.*   grocery story
aller *(m.)* simple   one-way (ticket)
aller-retour *m.*   round-trip (ticket)
aller   go; feel; suit
alors   well, then
ambulance *f.*   ambulance
ami(e) *m., f.*   friend
amour *m.*   love
s'amuser   enjoy o.self
an *m.*, année *f.*   year
annuaire *m.*   telephone book
annuel/le   annual
appareil *m.*   telephone;
   —photo   camera
appeler   call; s'—   be named
apporter   bring
après   after
après-midi   afternoon
arbre *m.*   tree
architecte *m.*   architect
argent *m.*   money
s'arranger   be settled
arrêt *(m.)* d'autobus   bus stop
arriver   arrive; happen
ascenseur *m.*   elevator
assez   enough, quite
s'asseoir   sit down
assiette *f.*   plate, dish
assister (à)   be present (at)
assurance *f.*   insurance
atteindre   reach

attendre   wait for
au-dessous   below
au-dessus   above
auberge *(f.)* de jeunesse   youth hostel
aujourd'hui   today
au revoir   good-bye
aussi   too, as well
autre   other
auto *m.*   car
autobus *m.*   bus
autoroute *f.*   highway
avance: à l'—   in advance; d'—   early
avec   with
averse *f.*   shower (rain)
avion *m.*   airplane
avis: à mon—   in my opinion
avoir   have

bagages *m. pl.*   luggage
balcon *m.*   balcony
banane *f.*   banana
banque *f.*   bank
barquette *f.*   carton
bateau *m.*   boat
batiment *m.*   building
beau, belle, bel   beautiful, good, etc.
beaucoup   very much; a lot
besoin: avoir—de   need
beurre *m.*   butter
bicyclette *f.*   bicycle
bien   well; —sûr   of course
bientôt   soon
bière *f.*   beer
bifteck *m.*   steak
billet *m.*   ticket; bill (money)
blanc(he)   white
blessé   hurt, injured
bleu   blue; very rare; *(m.)* bruise
blouson *m.*   (short) jacket
bœuf *m.*   beef
boire   drink
bois *m.*   wood
boisson *f.*   drink
boîte *f.*   box, can; —aux lettres
   mailbox; —de nuit   night club
bon(ne)   good; —marché   cheap
bonjour   hello
de bonne heure   early
boucherie *f.*   butcher shop
boulangerie *f.*   bakery
bouteille *f.*   bottle
bras *m.*   arm
brosse *f.*   brush

brouillard *m.* fog
brume *f.* mist
brun brown
Bruxelles Brussels
bureau *m.* office; —de change
  currency exchange; —de poste
  post office; —de tabac tobacco store
bulletin *(m.)* météorologique
weather forecast

ça that
cabine *(f.)* téléphonique phone booth
cabinet *(m.)* de toilette toilet
café *m.* coffee, café
caisse *f.* cashier
caisser *m.* cashier
calmant *m.* painkiller
se calmer calm down
campagne *f.* country
camarade *m., f.* friend
camion *m.* truck
camping *m.* camping, campground
car *m.* bus, coach
carafe *f.* jug
caravane *f.* trailer
carnet *m.* book of tickets; —de
  chèques checkbook; —de
  timbres book of stamps
carotte *f.* carrot
carrefour *m.* crossroads
carte *f.* menu, map, card;
  —bancaire bank card;
  —de crédit credit card; —postale
  postcard; —des vins wine list
cas *m.* case
cassé broken
casse-croûte *m.* snack
catastrophe *f.* catastrophe
cause: à—de because of
ce cette, cet this, that
cela that
celui-ci this one; celui-là that one
centre *m.* center
cerise *f.* cherry
ces these, those
c'est it is
chambre *f.* room
changer change, exchange
chapeau *m.* hat
chaque each
charcuterie *f.* delicatessen
chariot *m.* cart
chasser chase
château *m.* castle

chaud warm
chaussures *f. pl.* shoes
chemin *m.* way, road; —de
  fer railroad
chemise *f.* shirt
chemisier *m.* blouse
chèque *m.* check; —s de voyage/
  travellers traveler's checks
cher/chère expensive, dear
chercher look for
chéri(e) *m., f.* darling
chez at the home of
chic smart
chocolat *m.* chocolate
choisir choose
choix *f.* choice
chômeur/se *m.,f.* unemployed person
chose *f.* thing
cidre *m.* cider
ciel *m.* sky
cigarette *f.* cigarette
cinéma *m.* movies
circulation *f.* traffic
citron *m.* lemon
classe *f.* class
clé *f.* key
cœur *m.* heart
coffre *m.* trunk
coiffeur *m.* hairdresser
colis *m.* parcel
collège *m.* high school
collègue *m., f.* colleague
combien how much, how many
commander order
comme as, like
commencer begin
comment how
commissariat *(m.)* de police police
  station
complet full; —*(m.)* man's suit
complètement completely
comprendre understand
comprimé *m.* tablet, pill
compris included
concert *m.* concert
conducteur/trice *m., f.* driver
confiserie *f.* candy store
confiture *f.* jam
confortable comfortable
connaissance *f.* acquaintance
connaître know
conseiller advise
consigne *f.* luggage storage;
  —automatique locker

constat *m.* accident report
consulter consult
continuer continue
contravention *f.* fine
contre against
copain *m.,* copine *f.* friend, pal
correspondance *f.* connection
côte *f.* coast; rib
côté: à—de next to, beside
côtelette *f.* chop, cutlet
coton *m.* cotton
cou *m.* neck
se coucher go to bed
couleur *f.* color
coupé cut
courrier *m.* mail
court short
cousin(e) *m., f.* cousin
couteau *m.* knife
coûter cost
couvert overcast, covered;
 —(m.) place setting
couverture *f.* blanket
crème *f.* cream
crémerie *f.* dairy
crevettes *f. pl.* shrimps
crise *f.* crisis; —de foie upset stomach
croire think, believe
cuillère *f.* spoon
cuisine *f.* kitchen; faire la— cook
cuisiner cook
cuisinier/ière *m., f.* cook
cuir *m.* leather

dame *f.* lady
danger *m.* danger
dans in
danse *f.* dance
de of, from; some, any
début *m.* beginning
défendu, défense de forbidden (to)
déjà already
déjeuner *m.* lunch; petit— breakfast
demain tomorrow
demander ask for
démarrer start (car)
demi half; —heure *f.* half an hour;
 —pension *f.* half board
dent *f.* tooth
dentifrice *m.* toothpaste
dentiste *m., f.* dentist
départ *m.* departure
se dépêcher hurry
depuis since

dernier/ère last
des some, any
descendre get off, go down
désirer want
désolé sorry
dessert *m.* dessert
dessinateur *m.* designer
destination *f.* destination
détester hate, detest
devenir become
devoir have to, must
Dieu *m.* God
difficile difficult
dîner *m.* dinner, supper; — dine
dire say
direction *f.* direction
discuter discuss
disque *(m.)* de stationnement
 parking disk
docteur *m.* doctor
doigt *m.* finger
dommage *m.* pity, shame
donner give
dormir sleep
dos *m.* back
douane *f.* customs
douche *f.* shower
douloureux/se painful
doute: sans— no doubt
douzaine *f.* dozen
dresser put up (tent)
droguerie *f.* hardware store
droite right
du, de la, de l' some, any

eau *f.* water
école *f.* school
écrevisse *f.* crayfish, prawn
écrire write
égal: ça m'est— I don't care;
 également equally, likewise
église *f.* church
elle she
emballer wrap (up)
emmener take
emplacement *m.* campsite
employé(e) *m., f.* employee;
 —de banque bank teller
en in; some
encaisser cash (check)
enfant *m., f.* child
ennuyer bore
entrée *f.* entrance
entrer enter

VOCABULARY

environ   around about
envoyer   send
erreur *f.*   mistake
escalier *m.*   staircase
escargot *m.*   snail
espérer   hope
essayer   try (on)
essence *f.*   gas
étage *m.*   story, floor
étroit   tight, narrow
étudiant(e) *m., f.*   student
étudier   study
études: faire des—   study
envie: avoir—de   want
exposition *f.*   exhibition

face: en—de   across from
faim *f.*   hunger; avoir—   be hungry
faire   do, make; —beau   be nice
   (weather); ça fait   that comes to
farine *f.*   flour
faut: il—   be necessary, (I etc.) must
faute *f.*   fault
femme *f.*   woman, wife
fermer   close; fermé   closed
fermeture *f.*   closure
feux *m. pl.*   traffic lights
fiche *f.*   form
fièvre *f.*   fever, temperature
filet *m.*   net
fille *f.*   girl, daughter
film *m.*   film; —policier   thriller
fils *m.*   son
fin *f.*   end
finir   finish
flatteur/se   flattering
foie *m.*   liver
fois *f.*   time
forêt *f.*   forest
formulaire *m.*   form
fourchette *f.*   fork
frais/fraîche   fresh
fréquent   frequent
fraise *f.*   strawberry
framboise *f.*   raspberry
freins *m. pl.*   brakes
frites *f. pl.*   french fries
froid   cold
fromage *m.*   cheese
fruit *m.*   fruit
fumer   smoke

gâché   ruined
galerie, seconde *f.*   second balcony

garage *m.*   garage
garçon *m.*   boy, waiter
gardien/ne *m., f.*   warden
gare *f.*   station
gasoil *m.*   diesel
gâteau *m.*   cake
gauche   left
gaz *m.*   gas
geler   freeze
général: en—   in general
genou(x) *m. (pl.)*   knee(s)
gentil(le)   nice, kind
gilet *m.*   jacket, vest
glace *f.*   ice cream; glass
gonflé   swollen
gorge *f.*   throat
gourmand   greedy
goût *m.*   taste
goûter   taste; —(m.)   afternoon snack
gramme *m.*   gram
grand   large, big; —s magasins *m. pl.*
   department store; —mère *f.*
   grandmother; —père *m.*
   grandfather
gratuit   free
grave   serious
grêle *f.*   hail
grenouille *f.*   frog
gris   grey
grillé   grilled
gueule *(f.)* de bois   hangover
guichet *m.*   ticket office, counter
guide *m.*   guide, guidebook
guitare *f.*   guitar

habiter   live
heure *f.*   hour; —s   o'clock; —s
   d'ouverture   opening hours
heureux/se   happy, fortunate
hier   yesterday
homard *m.*   lobster
homme *m.*   man
hôpital *f.*   hospital
horaire *m.*   schedule
horreur: avoir—de   hate
hors d'œuvre *m.*   appetizer
hôtel *m.*   hotel; —de ville   town hall
huile *f.*   oil; —solaire   suntan lotion
huître *f. pl.*   oysters

ici   here
idée *f.*   idea
idiot   stupid
il   he, it; —y a   there is, there are

VOCABULARY

île f. island
immédiatement immediately
imperméable m. raincoat
infirmière f. nurse
s'inquiéter worry, be worried
instant m. moment, instant
instrument m. instrument
intéressant interesting
intéresser interest; s'—(à) be
  interested (in)
interdit, interdiction de forbidden (to)
isolé isolated
inviter invite

jambe f. leg
jambon m. ham
jardin m. garden
jeton m. token
joindre join, enclose
joli pretty
jouer play, show (film)
jour m. day; —s fériés (public)
  holidays; tous les —s every day
journal m. newspaper
jupe f. skirt
jus m. juice
jusqu'à to, until
juste just, right

kilo m. kilo(gram)
kiosque m. newsstand

la the, it
là there; —bas over there
lac m. lake
laine f. wool
laisser leave
lait m. milk
laitue f. lettuce
lame (f.) à raser razor blade
langoustine f. prawn
langue f. language; tongue
le the, it
légumes m. pl. vegetables
lent slow; lentement slowly
les the, them
lettre f. letter
leur their
se lever get up
librairie f. bookstore
libre free; —service self-service
ligne f. line
limonade f. soda
lire read

litre m. liter
livre f. pound; —(m.) book
location f. (de voitures) (car) rental
loin far
Londres London
long(ue) long
longer go along
longtemps long, a long time
louer rent
lumière f. light
lunettes f. pl. glasses

ma my
madame madam, Mrs.
mademoiselle Miss
magasin m. shop
maillot (m.) de bain bathing suit
main f. hand
maintenant now
mairie f. town hall
mais but
maison f. house, home; —de
  commerce firm
mal: j'ai—à . . . my . . . hurts
malade ill
maladroit clumsy
manger eat
manteau m. coat
marchand(e) m., f. vendor
marché m. market
marcher walk, work (function)
mari m. husband
marron (chestnut) brown
match m. (de football) (soccer) game
matin m. morning
mauvais bad
médecin m. doctor
médicament m. medicine
meilleur better, best
menu m. set meal, fixed-price menu
mer f. sea
merci thank you
mère f. mother
message m. message
messieurs m. gentlemen
mesurer measure
météo f. forecast
mètre m. meter
métro m. subway
midi noon
mieux better
minuit midnight
minute f. minute
mode: à la— fashionable

moi me
moins less
mois *m.* month
mon, ma, mes my
monnaie *f.* change
monsieur *m.* gentleman, Mr.
montagne *f.* mountain
monter go up
montre *f.* watch
montrer show
morceau *m.* piece
morue *f.* cod
mouchoir *m.* handkerchief
moules *f. pl.* mussels
moulu ground
musée *m.* museum; **–d'art** art gallery
musique *f.* music

nager swim
nationalité *f.* nationality
nature plain
ne . . . jamais never; ne . . . pas
  not; ne . . . personne no one; ne
  . . . plus no longer; ne . . . que
  only; ne . . . rien nothing
nécessaire necessary
neige *f.* snow
ni nor
noir black
nom *m.* last name
non no
nos our
note *f.* bill
notre our
nous we, us
nouveau/elle/el new
nuage *m.* cloud
nuageux cloudy
nuit *f.* night
numéro *m.* number; **–de téléphone**
  phone number
nylon *m.* nylon

occuper occupy; occupé busy
œil, yeux *m., pl.* eye, eyes
œuf *m.* egg
œuvre *f.* (d'art) work (of art)
oignon *m.* onion
ombre *f.* shadow
omelette *f.* omelet
orage *m.* storm
orange *m.* orange
orchestre: à l'– ground floor
ordinaire regular (gas)

ordonnace *f.* prescription
oreille *f.* ear
oreiller *m.* pillow
ou or
où where
oublier forget
oui yes
ouvrir open; ouvert open
ouvre-boîtc *m.* can opener
ouvre-bouteille *m.* bottle opener
ouvreuse *f.* usher

page *f.* page
paille *f.* straw
pain *m.* bread
panne *f.* breakdown
panser dress, bandage
pantalon *m.* pants
papa Dad
papeterie *f.* stationery store
paquet *m.* pack
par by; **–ici** this way
parapluie *m.* umbrella
parc *m.* park
paresseux/se lazy
parfait perfect
parfum *m.* perfume
parking *m.* parking lot
parler speak
part: de la–de on behalf of
partie *f.* part
partir depart, go away
partenaire *m., f.* partner
pas not; **–du tout** not at all
passeport *m.* passport
passer pass, go, spend; **–des radios**
  take some X rays
pâté *m.* (de campagne) pâté
pâtisserie *f.* pastry shop
payer pay
pays *m.* country
péage *m.* (road) toll
pêche *f.* peach; fishing
peigne *m.* comb
pellicule *f.* film
pendant during
penser think
pension *(f.)* complète full board
père *m.* father
perdre lose
permettre allow, permit
permis *(m.)* de conduire driver's
  license
personne *f.* person

VOCABULARY

petit little; –déjeuner *m.* breakfast;
 –pain *m.* roll; –s pois *m. pl.* peas
peu little
phare *f.* headlight
pharmacie *f.* pharmacy
pharmacien(ne) *m., f.* pharmacist
photographie *f.* photo, photography
pièce *f.* coin
pied *m.* foot; à– on foot
pile *f.* battery
piquer string
piscine *f.* swimming pool
place *f.* square; seat
plage *f.* beach
plaire please; ça me plaît I like it
plaisir *m.* pleasure
plan *m.* street map
planche *(f.)* à voile windsurfer
plaquette *f.* slab (butter)
plat *m.* dish, course: –cuisiné
 carryout food
plateau *(m.)* de fromage cheese tray
plein full; faites le– fill it up (car)
pleut: il– it's raining
pluie *f.* rain
plus more
plusieurs several
plutôt rather
pneu *m.* tire
poêle *f.* (frying) pan
poids lourds *m. pl.* heavy vehicles
poignet *m.* wrist
pointure *f.* size (shoe)
poire *f.* pear
poisson *m.* fish
poissonnerie *f.* fish market
poivre *m.* pepper
police *f.* police; policy; –d'assurance
 insurance policy
pommade *f.* ointment
pomme *f.* apple; –de terre *f.*
 potato
pompiste *m., f.* gas station attendant
pont *m.* bridge
porc *m.* pork
porcelaine *f.* porcelain, china
port *m.* port, harbor
porte *f.* door
porter carry, wear
porte-monnaie *m.* change purse
portefeuille *m.* wallet
poste *f.* post (office); bureau *(m.)*
 de– post office
poste *m.* extension (tel.)

potage *m.* soup
poudre: en– granulated
poulet *m.* chicken
pour for, in order to
pourboire *m.* tip
pourquoi why
pousser push
pouvoir be able, can
préférer prefer
premier first; –secours *m.* first aid
prendre take
prénom *m.* first name
près de near
présenter introduce, present; se–
 introduce o.self
président *m.* president
pression *f.* pressure; draft beer
prévoir foresee, forecast
prix *m.* price, prize
professeur *m., f.* teacher
produit *m.* product
programmeur/se *m., f.* computer
 programmer
promenade *f.* walk
pull(over) *m.* pullover sweater
puis then

quai *m.* platform
quand when
quart *m.* quarter
que what, which, that
quel, quelle which, that, what
quelque chose something, anything
quelques a few
quelqu'un someone
qu'est-ce que c'est? what is it?
qu'est-ce qu'il y a? what's the matter?
qui who
quincaillerie *f.* hardware (store)
quitter leave

raisin *m.* grape
râpé grated
rapide *m.* high-speed train
raser shave
rasoir *m.* razor
réception *f.* reception
recommander recommend
réchaud *m.* stove
réduction *f.* reduction
réduit reduced
regarder look at
région *f.* region, district
règlement *m.* payment

regretter regret
rejoindre join
remède *m.* remedy
remercier thank
remplir fill in
rencontrer meet; **rencontre** *m.*
  meeting
rendez-vous *m.* appointment
renseignements *m. pl.* information
se renseigner enquire
repas *m.* meal
répéter repeat
se reposer rest
représentant *m.* sales representative
réserver reserve
restaurant *m.* restaurant
rester stay
retard: en— late
retourner return; **retour** *m.* return
rez-de-chaussée *m.* ground floor
rhume *m.* cold
rivière *f.* river
riz *m.* rice
robe *f.* dress
rognons *m. pl.* kidneys
rose pink
rôti roast
roue *f.* wheel
rouge red
route *f.* road
rue *f.* street

sac *m.* (hand)bag; **—de couchage**
  sleeping bag
saignant rare
saison *m.* season
salade *f.* lettuce, salad
salaire *m.* salary
salle *f.* room; **—d'attente** waiting
  room; **—de bains** bathroom; **—de**
  concert concert hall
salut hello
sans without
saucisse *f.* sausage
saucisson *m.* (salami-type) sausage
saumon *m.* salmon
sauver save
savoir know
savon *m.* soap
séance *m.* showing, session
secours *m.* help; **au—!** help!
secrétaire *m., f.* secretary
sel *m.* salt

semaine *f.* week
sens unique one-way street
se sentir feel
service *m.* service; **—de dépannage**
  road service
serviette *f.* napkin; **—de bain** bath
  towel; **—hygiénique** sanitary napkin
seul alone, only; **seulement** only
shampooing *m.* shampoo
si if
signaler report
signe *f.* sign
signer sign
soif *f.* thirst; **avoir—** be thirsty
s'il vous plaît please
ski *m.* skiing; **—nautique**
  waterskiing
slip *m.* underpants
soie *f.* silk
soir *m.* **soirée** *f.* evening
soleil *m.* sun
son, sa, ses his, her
sortie *f.* exit; **—de secours**
  emergency exit
sortir go out
soupe *f.* soup
sous under
souvent often
sparadrap *m.* adhesive bandage
spécialité *f.* specialty
spectacle *m.* entertainment, show
stade *m.* stadium
standardiste *m., f.* operator
station *(f.)* **de métro** subway station
stationnement *m.* parking
stationner park
station-service *f.* service station
sucre *m.* sugar
super super (gas)
supermarché *m.* supermarket
superbe superb
sur on
surprise *f.* surprise
survêtement *m.* sweatsuit
surveillé guarded, supervised
syndicat d'initiative *m.* tourist
  information office

tabac *m.* tobacco; **bureau** *(m.)* **de—**
  tobacco store
table *f.* table
taille *f.* size, waist
tailleur *m.* woman's suit

tard   late
tarte *f.*   pie; **−aux pommes**   apple pie
tasse *f.*   cup
taux *(m.)* de change   exchange rate
taxi *m.*   taxi
tee-shirt *m.*   T-shirt
téléphoner   telephone
température *f.*   temperature
temps *m.*   time, weather; **à−**   on time
   (train); **à mi−**   part-time
tentation *f.*   temptation
tente *f.*   tent
terrain *(m.)* de camping
   campground
tête *f.*   head; **−en l'air**   scatterbrain
thé *m.*   tea
théâtre *m.*   theater
thon *m.*   tuna
tiens!   so, well!
timbre *m.*   stamp; **timbré**   stamped
tir *(m.)* à l'arc   archery
tire-bouchon *m.*   corkscrew
tirer   pull
toilettes *f. pl.*   toilets
tomate *f.*   tomato
tomber   fall
ton, ta, tes   your
tort: en−   in the wrong
toucher   touch
toujours   always
tour *f.*   tower
tourner   turn
tournevis *m.*   screwdriver
tousser   cough
tout   all; **−droit**   straight ahead; **−le
   monde**   everyone; **à−e à l'heure**
   see you soon; **−près**   near, nearby
toutefois   however
train *m.*   train
tranche *f.*   slice
travail *m.*   work; **travaux *pl.***   road
   repair
travailler   work
traverser   cross
très   very
tricostéril *m.*   bandage
trop (de)   too (much)
trouver   find; **se−**   be found/situated
truite *f.*   trout

un, une   a, an
usine *f.*   factory

vacances *f. pl.*   vacation

valise *f.*   suitcase
varier   vary
veau *m.*   veal
vélo *m.*   bicycle
velours *m.*   velvet
vendeur/se *m., f.*   salesperson
vendre   sell
venir   come
vent *m.*   wind
vente *f.*   sale, selling
ventre *m.*   stomach
verglas *m.*   ice, icy road
vérifier   check
verre *m.*   glass; **−de contact**
   contact lens
vert   green
veste *f.*   jacket
vêtements *m. pl.*   clothes
viande *f.*   meat
vieux/vieille/vieil   old
ville *f.*   town
violon *m.*   violin
vin *m.*   wine
vinaigre *m.*   vinegar
virage *m.*   bend
visite *f.*   visit; **visiter**   visit
vite   quick, quickly
voici   here is/are
voie *f.*   track
voilà   there is/are
voile *f.*   sail, sailing
voilier *m.*   sailboat
voir   see
voiture *f.*   car
vol *m.*   theft, flight
volaille *f.*   poultry
voler   steal
voleur *m.*   thief
volontiers   willingly
votre, vos   your
vouloir   wish, want
vous   you
voyage *m.*   journey
voyons   let's see
vrai   true; **vraiment**   really, truly
vue *f.*   view

wagon-lit *m.*   sleeping car
wagon-restaurant *m.*   dining car

y   there
yaourt *m.*   yogurt

zone *(f.)* bleue   restricted parking